Southern Living

Off the Eaten Path

Second Helpings

Morgan Murphy

Southern Living

Off the
Eaten Path
Second
Helpings

Morgan Murphy

Oxmoor
House.

ISBN-13: 978-0-8487-3955-3
ISBN-10: 0-8487-3955-8
Library of Congress Control Number: 2013932017

Printed in the United States of America
Third Printing 2014

Oxmoor House
Editorial Director: Leah McLaughlin
Creative Director: Felicity Keane
Senior Brand Manager: Daniel Fagan
Senior Editor: Rebecca Brennan
Managing Editor: Rebecca Benton

Off the Eaten Path: Second Helpings
Editor: Nichole Aksamit
Art Director: Claire Cormany
Project Editor: Megan McSwain Yeatts
Senior Designer: Melissa Clark
Director, Test Kitchen: Elizabeth Tyler Austin
Assistant Directors, Test Kitchen: Julie Christopher, Julie Gunter
Recipe Developers and Testers: Wendy Ball, R.D.; Victoria E. Cox; Tamara Goldis; Stefanie Maloney; Callie Nash; Karen Rankin; Leah Van Deren
Recipe Editor: Alyson Moreland Haynes
Food Stylists: Margaret Monroe Dickey, Catherine Crowell Steele
Photography Director: Jim Bathie
Senior Photographer: Hélène Dujardin
Senior Photo Stylist: Kay E. Clarke
Photo Stylist: Mindi Shapiro Levine
Assistant Photo Stylist: Mary Louise Menendez
Senior Production Manager: Susan Chodakiewicz
Production Manager: Terri Beste-Farley

Time Home Entertainment Inc.
Publisher: Jim Childs
VP, Strategy & Business Development: Steven Sandonato
Executive Director, Marketing Services: Carol Pittard
Executive Director, Retail & Special Sales: Tom Mifsud
Director, Bookazine Development & Marketing: Laura Adam
Executive Publishing Director: Joy Butts
Associate Publishing Director: Megan Pearlman
Finance Director: Glenn Buonocore
Associate General Counsel: Helen Wan

Southern Living®
Editor: M. Lindsay Bierman
Creative Director: Robert Perino
Managing Editor: Candace Higginbotham
Art Director: Chris Hoke
Executive Editors: Rachel Hardage Barrett, Hunter Lewis, Jessica S. Thuston
Food Director: Shannon Sliter Satterwhite
Test Kitchen Director: Rebecca Kracke Gordon
Senior Writer: Donna Florio
Senior Food Editor: Mary Allen Perry
Recipe Editor: JoAnn Weatherly
Assistant Recipe Editor: Ashley Arthur
Test Kitchen Specialist/Food Styling: Vanessa McNeil Rocchio
Test Kitchen Professionals: Norman King, Pam Lolley, Angela Sellers
Senior Photographers: Ralph Lee Anderson, Gary Clark, Art Meripol
Photographers: Robbie Caponetto, Laurey W. Glenn
Photo Research Coordinator: Ginny P. Allen
Senior Photo Stylist: Buffy Hargett
Editorial Assistant: Pat York

Contributors
Writer: Morgan Murphy
Recipe Developers and Testers: Erica Hopper, Tonya Johnson, Kyra Moncrief, Kathleen Royal Phillips
Copy Editors: Donna Baldone, Norma Butterworth-McKittrick
Proofreader: Donna Baldone, Adrienne Davis
Indexer: Mary Ann Laurens
Interns: Morgan Bolling, Susan Kemp, Alicia Lavender, Sara Lyon, Staley McIlwain, Jeffrey Preis, Emily Robinson, Maria Sanders, Julia Sayers
Food Stylist: Ana Kelly
Photographers: Ball & Albanese, Jennifer Davick, Beau Gustafson, Becky Luigart-Stayner, Morgan Murphy
Photo Stylists: Mary Clayton Carl, Missie Neville Crawford

Front Cover: Art Meripol

Contents

Y'all,

I've eaten my way across the South. I've pigged out at barbecue shacks, hamburger stands, meat-and-threes, taco trucks, juice bars, roadside dives, fish fries, juke joints, white-tablecloth restaurants, downtown diners, rustic old watering holes, trendy nightclubs, classic steak houses, and even a goat farm. I may be the only man in America who can qualify for workers' comp based on my cholesterol.

Know this: My picks here were researched the old-fashioned way, by finding restaurants based on word-of-mouth recommendations and covering 12,000 miles through 16 states and the District of Columbia. I've eaten everything in this book at least once, and these are my very favorites. Yep, a lot of it is fried, covered in butter, dripping with some kind of delicious sauce. This isn't a diet book. In fact, you may gain 30 pounds just *reading* it. But trust me, you'll discover a lot of the South's cutting-edge culinary delights in here, too. Not just the fried stuff.

Many of the cooks, chefs, and kitchen wizards whose genius graces these pages are on the forefront of the culinary arts. It helps that our region is graced with a huge assortment of farms, fisheries, dairies, vineyards, and other food producers. The South boasts excellent seafood and beef, amazing grains and citrus, and rich and rare produce of nearly every variety. Combined with a collision of English, Irish, Scottish, German, Caribbean, West African, French, Spanish, Native American, and Mexican history, that diversity gives the South a broad tapestry of restaurants you won't find anywhere else.

So, dig into Second Helpings—whip up a healthy juice smoothie, a not-so-healthy (but delish) hot dog, the best banana pudding on the planet, or the grape and rosemary pizza I can't stop dreaming about. I promise, you're likely to love these recipes. Why? They're not just dishes I whipped up in my own kitchen. No, these are secrets revealed for the first time and cherished recipes that keep these featured restaurants full of customers.

Can't cook? Don't sweat it. This book works for the kitchen-impaired as well. Simply hop in the car, as I did, and visit these restaurants for yourself. Hey, and if you find a great new spot, please tell me about it. (My Twitter handle is @_morganmurphy.) And to make your road trip even more fun, I've included some of my favorite hotels and soundtracks for you to enjoy along the way.

Eat up!

Morgan Murphy

Stockyard Cafe ↙

Lucky LAYLA FARMS
★ FARMS ★
Superior Handcrafted
Dairy Products

Lucky Layla
Farm Store at
Lavon Farms ↙

Salsa Fuego ↘

The Corner Market ↙

The Porch ↖

Coffee Shop Cafe ↓

Standpipe Coffee
House ↓

LONE STAR
BEER ®

LONE STAR BREWING COMPANY
SAN ANTONIO, TEXAS

Hillside Farmacy ↓

↙ Maxine's on Main

FROM the WEST

Texas • Oklahoma • Missouri

Rock Cafe
↙

Nic's Grill
↓

Abigail's
↓

Vintage Restaurant at Stone Hill Winery
↓

Coffee Shop Cafe

1005 West McGregor Drive
McGregor, Texas
(254) 840-2027

Unless you're related to Jessica Simpson, happen to be Governor Perry's personal pie-fetcher, or were a member of the White House Press Corps from 2000 to 2008, you probably don't know about this little coffee shop 20 minutes from Waco. Donald Citrano's menu is full of Texas classics such as migas, big ol' pancakes, cornbread salad, and fried everything. But forget all that. You're here for Valerie Citrano's pie. This little lady makes some big, big pies, adored by pop stars, potentates, and presidents. Valerie will tell you with a gleam in her eye who likes which pie, but take it from me, they're all delicious.

Coffee Shop Cafe Chocolate Cream Pie

Made with Valerie's grandmother's recipe, this pie is tremendous both in taste and height.

Pie

1	(9-inch) frozen unbaked piecrust shell
⅔	cup sugar
¼	cup all-purpose flour
2	Tbsp. unsweetened cocoa
⅛	tsp. salt
2	cups milk
3	egg yolks, lightly beaten
1	Tbsp. butter
½	tsp. vanilla extract

Mile-High Meringue

6	egg whites
¼	tsp. cream of tartar
¾	cup sugar
¼	tsp. vanilla extract
1	tsp. unsweetened cocoa

1. Prepare Pie: Bake piecrust shell according to package directions. Cool on a wire rack.

2. Meanwhile, place sugar, flour, cocoa, and salt in a medium saucepan; whisk in milk, and bring to a boil over medium-high heat, stirring constantly. Boil 1 minute, stirring constantly. Whisk egg yolks in a medium bowl until thick and pale. Gradually stir about one-fourth of hot milk mixture into yolks; add yolk mixture to remaining hot milk mixture, stirring constantly. Cook over medium heat, stirring constantly, 2 minutes or until pudding-like thickness. Remove from heat; stir in butter and vanilla. Cover and keep hot.

3. Prepare Mile-High Meringue: Preheat oven to 325°. Beat egg whites and cream of tartar at high speed with an electric mixer until foamy.

Add sugar, 1 Tbsp. at a time, beating until stiff peaks form and sugar dissolves (about 2 to 4 minutes). Beat in vanilla.

4. Pour hot pudding into piecrust shell. Spread meringue over hot pudding, sealing edges. Dust with cocoa. Bake at 325° for 20 minutes or until golden brown. Cool completely on a wire rack (about 2 hours). Cover loosely, and chill 4 hours or overnight before serving. For easy slicing, dip knife in hot water before each cut. Refrigerate leftovers–if there are any. **Makes 6 to 8 servings.**

Make it a Coconut Cream Pie: Omit cocoa. Add 1 cup sweetened flaked coconut with the butter and vanilla in Step 2. Assemble and bake pie as directed. Top with ¼ cup sweetened flaked coconut.

Coffee Shop Cafe Cornbread Salad

Sweet and savory, this could be considered a "salad" only in Texas.

1 cup all-purpose flour
1 cup plain yellow cornmeal
½ cup sugar
2 Tbsp. baking powder
¾ tsp. salt
1 cup plus 2 Tbsp. milk
¼ cup vegetable oil
2 large eggs
1¼ cups diced green bell pepper (1 medium)
1¼ cups diced red onion (1 medium)
1¼ cups seeded and diced tomato (2 medium)
1 cup mayonnaise
¾ cup cooked and crumbled bacon slices (8 slices)
¼ cup seeded and minced jalapeño pepper (2 medium)
½ tsp. salt
½ tsp. freshly ground pepper

1. Preheat oven to 425°. Stir together first 5 ingredients in a large bowl. Whisk together milk, oil, and eggs in a medium bowl; stir into flour mixture just until blended. (Don't overwork or cornbread will be dry.) Pour batter into a lightly greased 13- x 9-inch pan.
2. Bake at 425° for 20 minutes or until golden brown and a wooden pick inserted in center comes out clean. Cool cornbread completely (about 30 minutes).
3. Crumble cornbread into bite-size pieces into a large bowl. Add bell pepper and remaining ingredients, and toss well to coat. Cover and chill 4 hours or overnight for best flavor.
Makes 8 to 10 servings.

SOUNDTRACK:

"Elevator" by Texas beauty Erin McCarley

"Gather the Horses" by Charlie Mars

"I Will Wait" by Mumford & Sons

"Let It Be Me" by Ray LaMontagne

"Down by the Water" by The Decemberists

"Spring Wind" by Jack Johnson

The Corner Market

3426 Greenville Avenue
Dallas, Texas
(214) 826-8282

Every neighborhood needs a market like this, where you can stop in for a perfect cup of coffee or a quick lunch. The friendly staffers here dish out dozens of salads and sandwiches. A cake store and knickknack shop share adjoining spaces, so you can pick up a cupcake or a scented candle on the way out. But it's the people-watching here that's particularly captivating. Everyone in this "M streets" (so called because many of the nearby street names begin with the letter M) market is just so darned good-looking and stylish. Maybe it's something in those salads.

Corner Market Confetti Potato Salad

This is the most colorful potato salad I've ever seen—and one of the best I've tasted.

1¾	lb. unpeeled round red potatoes (about 10 potatoes)
1½	cups diced celery (4 ribs)
1	diced red bell pepper
1	diced yellow bell pepper
1	cup pitted black olives
1	cup pitted Spanish olives
¾	cup diced red onion (1 small)
1½	cups mayonnaise
⅓	cup chopped fresh flat-leaf parsley
¼	cup chopped fresh dill weed
¼	cup spicy sweet pickle relish
2½	Tbsp. refrigerated horseradish
2½	Tbsp. whole grain mustard
1	tsp. hot sauce
¼	tsp. salt
¼	tsp. freshly ground pepper

1. Cook potatoes in boiling salted water to cover 25 to 30 minutes or until tender; drain. Let cool completely.

2. Place potatoes in a large bowl; coarsely crush using hands. Add celery and next 5 ingredients. Stir together mayonnaise and remaining ingredients in a medium bowl. Add to potato mixture, stirring gently to coat. Cover and chill at least 2 hours before serving. **Makes 8 servings.**

Corner Market Texas Waldorf Salad

Crunchy and not too sweet, this classic salad is made dramatically better by the use of toasted pecans.

1   cup pecan halves
4   cups (1-inch) cubed unpeeled Granny Smith apple
2½ cups (1-inch) cubed peeled Bosc pears
1½ cups seedless green grapes
1½ cups seedless red grapes
2   Tbsp. coarsely chopped fresh flat-leaf parsley
1   cup dried cranberries
¾   cup bottled creamy poppy-seed dressing

1. Preheat oven to 350°. Bake pecans at 350° in a single layer in a shallow pan 5 to 6 minutes or until toasted and fragrant, stirring halfway through. Let cool completely.

2. Toss together apple and next 5 ingredients in a large bowl. Drizzle dressing over fruit mixture; sprinkle with nuts, and toss to coat. Cover and chill until serving, if desired. **Makes 10 servings.**

Hillside Farmacy

1209 East 11th Street
Austin, Texas
(512) 628-0168

I want to live here. Warm wooden cabinetry,
copper countertops, and 1920s-style tile
make this hip Austin spot a grand place to
settle in for a romantic evening out. The
Farmacy, so named because it's the site of
a former drugstore and it celebrates local
and fresh-from-the-farm ingredients, is also
a carnivore's delight. Chef and co-owner
Sonya Coté makes her own headcheese,
whips up amazing bison tartare, and speaks
of oysters with the familiarity and zeal that
Joan Rivers lavishes on red carpet fashion.
Medicate yourself with one of the Farmacy's
great cocktails, and prepare for a meal you
won't soon forget.

uncommon
OBJECTS

Hillside Farmacy Grapefruit Jalapeño Margarita

This spicy, smoky, salty twist on a Mexican classic will put some "git" in your gitalong. The coarse salts on the rim really make the drink. Look for them at specialty spice stores or online retailers such as thespicelab.com.

Lime wedge
Coarse Chihuahua de Mexico salt (smoked black salt)
Coarse Himalayan salt (pink salt)
3   Tbsp. jalapeño-infused tequila
2   Tbsp. orange liqueur
2   Tbsp. red grapefruit juice
½   tsp. fresh lime juice

1. Run lime wedge around the rim of a martini or margarita glass; dip half of rim in smoked black salt and half of rim in pink salt.
2. Combine tequila and next 3 ingredients in a cocktail shaker; add ice. Cover with lid, and shake vigorously until thoroughly chilled (30 seconds). Pour into prepared glass. **Makes 1 serving.**

Lavon Farms

Registered Guernseys

The Moores

Lucky Layla Farm Store at Lavon Farms

3721 North Jupiter Road
Plano, Texas
972-423-8080

I'm watching my glass of milk as the cream literally rises to the top. Lavon Farms sells raw milk straight from its Jersey and Guernsey cows. The difference from its grocery-store counterparts is nothing short of astonishing. The dairy also makes drinkable yogurt and delicious cheeses under the brand Lucky Layla, which is available throughout Dallas and at the Lucky Layla Farm Store at the dairy in Plano. Visitors are welcome at the farm, where award-winning cows amble in scenic pastures and the superclean milking room smells like an ice-cream parlor.

Lucky Layla Vanilla Ice Cream

Where to get the best ice-cream recipe? Straight from the dairy.

2   cups sugar
¼   cup plus 2 Tbsp. all-purpose flour
½   tsp. salt
6   cups milk
5   large eggs, lightly beaten
3   cups heavy cream
2   Tbsp. vanilla extract

1. Whisk together sugar, flour, and salt in a large heavy saucepan. Gradually whisk in milk; cook over medium heat, whisking constantly, 15 minutes or until thickened. Gradually whisk 2 cups hot milk mixture into eggs; gradually whisk egg mixture into remaining hot milk mixture, whisking constantly.

2. Cook over medium heat, whisking constantly, 2 minutes or until mixture slightly thickens.

3. Remove from heat; pour into a bowl. Fill a large bowl with ice. Place bowl containing milk mixture in ice, and let stand 2 hours or until chilled, stirring every 30 minutes. Stir in cream and vanilla.

4. Pour mixture into freezer container of a 1-gal. electric ice-cream maker, and freeze according to manufacturer's instructions. (Instructions and times may vary.)

5. Pour mixture into an airtight container, and freeze 2 hours or until firm. Let ice cream stand at room temperature 5 minutes to slightly soften before scooping. **Makes about 1 gal**.

Note: Lavon Farms uses a crank-style ice-cream maker with rock salt and ice. If you have a similar device, they advise filling the pail halfway with ice, adding 1 cup rock salt, filling the rest of the way with ice, and then adding 1 cup more rock salt before churning. (Too much salt causes the mixture to freeze too fast and creates a coarse, grainy texture, and not enough salt makes the ice cream more like butter.)

Lucky Layla Vanilla Caramels

These are creamy, chewy, and very soft.

2	Tbsp. butter, softened
2	cups sugar
2	cups whipping cream
¾	cup light corn syrup
½	cup butter
1	cup chopped black walnuts or pecans
1	tsp. vanilla extract

1. Grease a 9-inch square baking dish with softened butter. Stir together sugar, 1 cup cream, corn syrup, and ½ cup butter in a medium saucepan; bring to a boil over high heat, stirring constantly. Add remaining 1 cup cream gradually, so as not to stop the boiling process. Cook, stirring constantly, until a candy thermometer registers 246° or until drops of caramel form firm balls when dripped into cold water. Remove from heat; stir in nuts and vanilla.

2. Quickly spread caramel into prepared baking dish. Let cool completely (about 3 hours). Cover and let stand at room temperature 8 to 24 hours to set up. Cut into 1-inch squares, and wrap each caramel in wax paper. **Makes 80 caramels.**

The Farm Frappé: This light pick-me-up is a snap to make with a few of the caramels. Place 3 Lucky Layla Vanilla Caramels (or other 1-inch caramel squares) in a blender. Add ½ cup hot, freshly brewed dark-roast coffee. Let stand 1 minute to soften caramel. Add ½ cup of the freshest local milk you can find and 2 cups ice. Process into a frothy shake. **Makes 1 serving.**

Maxine's on Main

905 Main Street
Bastrop, Texas
(512) 303-0919

Main Street in tiny Bastrop looks like it came straight from a Hollywood back lot, and Maxine's on Main is exactly how you'd picture a Texas cafe. Pies, wagon wheel-size pancakes, chicken-fried steak, and big Mason jars of sweet tea make hungry diners here happy. For pure comfort food, try the pot roast. It's savory and rich, and its chuck-wagon secret ingredient is a full pot of coffee, which makes for an incredible and eye-opening gravy. Have a big piece of pie, and before you leave Bastrop be sure to amble around the few blocks of its downtown, which is full of quaint stores and historic buildings.

Maxine's Pot Roast

This is the darkest, richest pot roast I've ever tried. The restaurant makes a much larger batch, which uses a whole pot of coffee. We've scaled it down to a more reasonable home-kitchen size and put it in a slow cooker for even more ease.

- 2¼ tsp. freshly ground pepper, divided
- 2½ tsp. garlic powder
- 1½ tsp. onion powder
- 1½ tsp. seasoned salt
- 1 (3-lb.) boneless chuck roast, trimmed
- 2 Tbsp. vegetable oil
- 3 medium-size red potatoes, quartered
- 2 celery ribs, coarsely chopped
- 1 large carrot, peeled and coarsely chopped
- 1 small onion, diced
- 3 cups strong, freshly brewed coffee
- ¼ cup Worcestershire sauce
- 1 Tbsp. browning-and-seasoning sauce (optional)
- 3 Tbsp. butter
- ⅓ cup all-purpose flour
- ¾ tsp. salt

1. Stir together 1½ tsp. pepper and next 3 ingredients in a small bowl; rub over roast. Brown roast 3 to 4 minutes on each side in hot oil in a large skillet over high heat. Place roast and potatoes in a 6-qt. slow cooker.

2. Sauté celery, carrot, and onion in hot drippings in skillet over medium-high heat 2 minutes. Add coffee, Worcestershire sauce, and, if desired, browning-and-seasoning sauce; cook 3 minutes, stirring to loosen particles from bottom of skillet. Pour mixture over roast and potatoes.

3. Cover and cook on LOW 8 hours or until roast and potatoes are fork-tender. Transfer roast and vegetables to a serving platter, reserving cooking liquid. Shred roast with two forks; cover and keep warm. Skim fat from cooking liquid.

4. Melt butter in a medium saucepan over medium-high heat; gradually whisk in flour. Gradually whisk in reserved cooking liquid. Add remaining ¾ tsp. pepper and ¾ tsp. salt. Bring to a boil; reduce heat, and simmer, stirring occasionally, 3 minutes or until thickened. Serve gravy with roast and vegetables. **Makes 4 to 6 servings.**

Note: We tested with Kitchen Bouquet browning-and-seasoning sauce.

Texas

The Porch

2912 North Henderson Avenue
Dallas, Texas
(214) 828-2916

Though The Porch's menu is full of Texas comfort foods such as macaroni and cheese and schnitzel, it's not the sort that hits you like a stagecoach. "I don't want people to go home and feel like they have to take a nap," says Cordon Bleu–trained chef Kenneth Hardiman. The decor puts you at ease. The restaurant's beamed ceiling, rich leather booths, and long, commodious bar have an upscale Western feel, kinda like the King Ranch edition of a Ford F-250. Indulge in a martini and some watermelon salad—refreshing accompaniments to an afternoon on the porch—or settle in for a meal with a cheese plate and terrific pork schnitzel.

The Porch Black and Blue Martini

It's more deep raspberry in color than black or blue, and it's so sweet, you'll hardly notice the alcohol.

6 fresh blueberries
6 fresh mint leaves
3 fresh blackberries
2 Tbsp. vodka
2 Tbsp. St. Germain elder-flower liqueur
1½ Tbsp. fresh lime juice
1½ Tbsp. Simple Syrup (at right)
2 Tbsp. club soda, chilled
Garnishes: fresh mint leaves, lime zest curl

1. Muddle first 3 ingredients in a cocktail shaker. Add vodka, next 3 ingredients, and ice to fill shaker. Cover, shake, and strain through a fine sieve into a chilled martini glass. Gently pour in club soda. **Makes 1 serving.**

Simple Syrup

1 cup sugar

1. Bring sugar and 1 cup water to a boil in a small saucepan over medium heat. Boil, stirring occasionally, 7 minutes or until sugar dissolves and mixture is clear. Let cool 10 minutes or to room temperature. Store, covered, in refrigerator for use in cocktails. **Makes 1⅛ cups.**

The Porch Watermelon Salad

The Porch uses yellow watermelon for a twist, but pink- or red-fleshed melon will do.

1 Tbsp. fresh orange juice
1 Tbsp. fresh lemon juice
1 Tbsp. fresh lime juice
1 Tbsp. Champagne vinegar
½ tsp. salt
½ tsp. freshly ground pepper
¾ tsp. honey
¼ cup grapeseed oil
4 cups (1-inch) cubed seedless yellow watermelon
2 cups grape tomatoes, halved
2 cups (8 oz.) crumbled feta cheese
2 cups peeled and seeded cucumber, cut on a bias
1 cup vertically sliced red onion
½ cup thinly sliced fresh basil
3 to 4 oz. prosciutto, coarsely chopped

1. Whisk together first 7 ingredients. Gradually whisk in oil until blended.
2. Toss together watermelon and next 4 ingredients in a large bowl. Add dressing, and toss gently to coat, just before serving. Top with basil and prosciutto. Serve with a slotted spoon. **Makes 8 servings.**

The Porch
Burrata Cheese Plate

Burrata is simply a looser mozzarella. It's ideal for spreading and terrific with Peach Chutney.

1   large garlic bulb
1   Tbsp. olive oil
1   (8-oz.) package burrata or fresh mozzarella
2   tsp. extra virgin olive oil
¼   tsp. coarse sea salt
⅛   tsp. freshly ground pepper
½   cup Peach Chutney (below)
Grilled baguette slices

1. Preheat oven to 425°. Cut off pointed end of garlic bulb; place bulb on a piece of aluminum foil, and drizzle with 1 Tbsp. olive oil. Fold foil to seal. Bake at 425° for 40 to 45 minutes or until golden brown; let cool 10 minutes.
2. Place burrata in a small serving dish; drizzle with 2 tsp. extra virgin olive oil, and sprinkle with salt and pepper. Serve with roasted garlic, Peach Chutney, and grilled baguette slices. To serve, squeeze pulp from garlic cloves, and spread onto bread; top with cheese and chutney. **Makes 6 servings.**

Peach Chutney

½   cup diced red onion
½   cup diced red bell pepper
1   Tbsp. minced garlic
2   tsp. vegetable oil
½   cup firmly packed light brown sugar
1   tsp. freshly ground black pepper
1   tsp. ground red pepper
½   cup red wine vinegar
3   cups peeled and diced fresh peaches (about 2 lb.)
Garnish: fresh oregano or small basil leaves

1. Sauté onion, bell pepper, and garlic in hot oil in a medium saucepan over medium heat 4 minutes or until onion becomes translucent. Add brown sugar, freshly ground black pepper, and ground red pepper; cook over medium heat 8 to 10 minutes or until mixture begins to thicken. Add vinegar; cook 5 minutes. Remove from heat; fold in peaches.
2. Process half of peach mixture in a food processor until smooth, stopping to scrape down sides as needed. Stir pureed peach mixture into remaining peach mixture. Transfer to a small bowl; cover and chill at least 2 hours. Store in refrigerator up to 3 weeks. **Makes 2¾ cups.**

The Porch Pork Schnitzel with Cauliflower Puree and Peach-Arugula Salad

This crispy take on a German classic is lighter than most.

¾   cup all-purpose flour
1¾   tsp. kosher salt, divided
1¼   tsp. freshly ground pepper, divided
⅓   cup milk
3   large eggs
2   cups panko (Japanese breadcrumbs)
¾   cup freshly grated Parmesan cheese
¼   cup chopped fresh parsley
2½   lb. boneless pork loin, cut into 6 slices
¾   cup Clarified Butter (page 43) or peanut oil
Cauliflower Puree (at right)
Peach-Arugula Salad (at right)

1. Combine flour, 1½ tsp. salt, and 1 tsp. pepper in a shallow bowl. In second bowl, whisk together milk and eggs. Combine panko and next 2 ingredients in a third bowl.

2. Place pork slices between 2 pieces of heavy-duty plastic wrap, and flatten to ¼-inch thickness using a flat side of a meat mallet or rolling pin. Dredge pork in flour mixture; dip in egg mixture, and dredge in panko mixture.

3. Heat ¼ cup Clarified Butter in a large skillet over medium heat. Add 2 pork slices. Cook until pork is browned and desired degree of doneness. Remove from pan, and drain on a wire rack over paper towels. Wipe skillet clean. Repeat twice with remaining butter and pork. Sprinkle pork with remaining ¼ tsp. salt and ¼ tsp. pepper.

4. Spoon about ½ cup Cauliflower Puree on each of 6 plates. Place 1 pork slice on top of each portion of puree. Top each pork slice with 1½ cups of Peach-Arugula Salad. Serve immediately. **Makes 6 servings.**

Cauliflower Puree

4   cups cauliflower florets (1 small head)
½   cup heavy cream
2   Tbsp. sliced shallots
1   Tbsp. chopped garlic
1   fresh thyme sprig
¼   tsp. kosher salt
Pinch of freshly ground pepper

1. Bring first 5 ingredients to a boil in a medium saucepan; cover, reduce heat, and simmer 20 minutes or until liquid almost evaporates and cauliflower is tender. Remove thyme sprig.

2. Process cauliflower mixture in a blender or food processor until smooth. Stir in salt and pepper. **Makes 6 servings.**

Peach-Arugula Salad

1   cup sugar
1   cup red wine vinegar
1   cup red onion slices
2   Tbsp. whole grain mustard
2   Tbsp. sherry vinegar
4   tsp. honey
2   Tbsp. vegetable oil
Salt and pepper to taste
6   cups baby arugula
2   cups fresh peach slices

1. Combine sugar and red wine vinegar in large saucepan. Bring to a simmer, stirring until sugar dissolves. Stir in onion; remove from heat, and let cool completely (about 1 hour).

2. Process mustard and next 2 ingredients in a blender until combined. With blender running, add oil in a slow, steady stream, processing until smooth. Season with salt and pepper to taste.

3. Drain onions, discarding vinegar mixture. Place arugula, peach slices, onion, and dressing in a large bowl; toss until coated. Serve immediately. **Makes 6 servings.**

Salsa Fuego

3520 Alta Mere Drive
Fort Worth, Texas
(817) 560-7888

If you visit my favorite Mexican spot in Fort Worth, you're going to think I'm crazy. The restaurant sports purple walls. It has a defunct drive-through. It used to be a KFC. All of this might lead you to believe that you're about to have a cheapo Mexican dinner. Wrong. Chef-owner Carlos Rodriguez creates astounding gourmet dishes using only fresh ingredients and traditional techniques. You won't find a can in his kitchen, and his menu is a collision of Western, Southwestern, and Mexican cuisines. From simple delights like the fresh margaritas to more complex masterpieces like the Mexican lasagna, these creations have earned Carlos a following among those who yearn for more than plain ol' Tex-Mex.

Salsa Fuego Chile con Queso

Don't try substituting milk for the water in this creamy and delicious dip or it will come apart.

1	poblano pepper
1	(16-oz.) package pasteurized prepared cheese product, cubed
¼	cup chopped ripe tomato
1	Tbsp. chopped onion
¼	tsp. ground red pepper
⅛	tsp. salt
⅛	tsp. freshly ground black pepper
1	Tbsp. vegetable oil
½	cup chopped roasted Hatch chiles or 1 (4-oz.) can chopped green chiles, undrained
¼	cup dry white wine

Tortilla chips

1. Broil poblano pepper on an aluminum foil-lined baking sheet 5 inches from heat 10 minutes on each side or until pepper looks blistered. Place pepper in a zip-top plastic freezer bag; seal and let stand 10 minutes to loosen skins. Peel pepper; remove and discard seeds. Dice pepper to measure ¼ cup.

2. Combine cheese and ⅔ cup water in a medium saucepan over medium-low heat, and cook, stirring constantly, 5 minutes or until cheese melts and mixture is smooth.

3. Sauté tomato, onion, ground red pepper, salt, and pepper in hot oil in a large skillet over high heat 1 to 2 minutes. Stir in green chiles and diced poblano pepper; cook 2 minutes or just long enough to warm through. Add wine, and cook 1 minute. Stir tomato mixture into cheese mixture. Serve with tortilla chips. **Makes 3 cups.**

Salsa Fuego Mexican Lasagna

This beautiful dish will surprise those who think they know Mexican food. To make it easier, roast the peppers for the two sauces and the picadillo at the same time in the same skillet.

New Mexico Red Chile Sauce (at right)
Poblano Cream Sauce (page 36)
Picadillo (page 36)
Vegetable oil
24   (6-inch) corn tortillas
I   cup (4 oz.) shredded colby-Jack cheese blend
¼   cup diced yellow onion
Shredded lettuce, diced tomato, crumbled feta cheese

1. Prepare New Mexico Red Chile Sauce, Poblano Cream Sauce, and Picadillo. Keep warm.
2. Pour oil to depth of ½ inch in a deep skillet or Dutch oven; heat to 350°. Fry tortillas, in batches, 30 seconds or just until lightly browned. Drain on paper towels.
3. Spoon ½ cup Poblano Cream Sauce onto each of 8 plates. Place 1 tortilla on each plate; top each tortilla with 1 Tbsp. New Mexico Red Chile Sauce, 3 Tbsp. Picadillo, 1 Tbsp. cheese blend, and ¾ tsp. diced onion. Repeat layers once using tortillas, New Mexico Red Chile Sauce, Picadillo, cheese blend, and onion, stacking tortillas like pancakes. Top with remaining tortillas and New Mexico Red Chile Sauce. Drizzle remaining Poblano Cream Sauce over each serving. Top with shredded lettuce, diced tomato, and crumbled feta cheese. **Makes 8 servings.**

New Mexico Red Chile Sauce

I   lb. fresh New Mexico red chile peppers or red jalapeño peppers, halved and seeded
¼   cup ground cumin
2   Tbsp. dried Mexican oregano
I   tsp. kosher salt
3   garlic cloves, halved

1. Bring 6 cups water to a boil in a large saucepan. Meanwhile, roast peppers in a cast-iron skillet over high heat 1 to 2 minutes or just until skins begin to blister, turning once. Remove quickly,

OVERHEARD: "He's all hat and no cattle."

When I don my favorite Lucchese boots and straw Stetson, I look like I might have come straight from the ranch. Truth is, I couldn't rustle a five-year-old out of a Toys "R" Us parking lot. I reckon that's what's meant by this phrase you hear all over the great state of Texas.

and be careful not to burn them. (If the chiles turn black, they become bitter.) Place peppers in boiling water; reduce heat, and simmer 10 minutes. Remove from heat; cover and steep 20 minutes. Drain peppers, reserving ½ cup cooking liquid.

2. Process reserved ½ cup cooking liquid, peppers, cumin, oregano, salt, and garlic in a blender until smooth. Pour mixture through a fine wire-mesh strainer into saucepan. Cook over medium-high heat 2 to 3 minutes or until thoroughly heated. Remove from heat. Cover and keep warm; if not using immediately, cover and chill, and reheat when ready to use. **Makes 1½ cups.**

Poblano Cream Sauce

1   lb. poblano peppers
½   cup butter
¾   cup all-purpose flour
4   cups milk
¾   tsp. kosher salt
½   tsp. freshly ground black pepper
¼   tsp. ground nutmeg
6   garlic cloves, minced
1   Tbsp. vegetable oil
½   cup dry white wine
¼   cup (1 oz.) shredded Monterey Jack cheese

1. Roast poblano peppers in a cast-iron skillet over high heat, turning frequently, until skins are blackened and blistered on all sides, about 4 minutes per side. Place peppers in a large zip-top plastic freezer bag; seal and let stand 10 minutes to loosen skins. Peel peppers; remove and discard seeds. Cut peppers into thin strips.
2. Melt butter in a medium-size heavy saucepan over low heat; whisk in flour until smooth. Cook 1 minute, whisking constantly. Gradually whisk in milk; cook over medium heat, whisking constantly, until mixture is thickened and bubbly (about 4 minutes). Stir in salt, black pepper, and nutmeg. Remove from heat; keep warm.
3. Sauté garlic in hot oil in a large skillet over medium heat 1 minute. Add poblano pepper strips, and sauté 2 minutes. Add wine, and cook 2 minutes. Add poblano pepper mixture and cheese to cream sauce; cook over medium heat 1 minute, stirring constantly, until cheese melts. Remove from heat. Cover and keep warm. If not using within 2 hours, cover and chill; reheat when ready to use. **Makes 5¼ cups.**

Picadillo

6   to 8 jalapeño peppers
1   lb. ground round
½   cup diced yellow onion
2   garlic cloves, minced
1   Tbsp. paprika
1   Tbsp. ground cumin
2   tsp. kosher salt

1. Roast jalapeño peppers in a cast-iron skillet over high heat, turning frequently, until skins blister (about 3 minutes per side). Place peppers in a zip-top plastic freezer bag; seal and let stand 10 minutes to loosen skins. Peel; remove and discard seeds. Chop peppers to measure ⅓ cup.
2. Brown ground beef in a large skillet over medium-high heat, stirring often, 2 to 5 minutes or until meat crumbles and is no longer pink; drain. Return beef to skillet. Add onion and garlic; cook 5 minutes or until onion is tender, stirring often. Add ⅓ cup roasted jalapeño peppers, ½ cup water, paprika, cumin, and salt. Reduce heat, and simmer, uncovered, 10 minutes or until most of liquid evaporates. Remove from heat. Cover and keep warm; if not using immediately, cover, chill, and reheat when ready to use. **Makes 3 cups.**

Salsa Fuego 'Rita

This tart margarita is one of the best I've ever had.

⅔ cup Simple Syrup (page 27)

1½ cups fresh lime juice (8 large)

½ cup fresh lemon juice (3 large)

1 cup fresh orange juice (2 large)

5 lime wedges

Coarse margarita salt

¾ cup tequila

½ cup orange liqueur

1. Stir together Simple Syrup and juices in a ½-gal. pitcher, and chill until serving.

2. Run a lime wedge around the rim of 4 (12-oz.) glass mugs; dip rims of mugs in margarita salt to coat. Place in freezer to chill, if desired.

3. To serve, pour 1 cup juice mixture, 3 Tbsp. tequila, and 2 Tbsp. orange liqueur into each mug; gently stir (do not disturb salt rim). Fill mugs with ice. Place a lime wedge on rim of each mug. **Makes 4 servings.**

Standpipe Coffee House

123 South First Street
Lufkin, Texas
(936) 632-7473

I found this mecca of java quite by accident while exhausted and lost in Lufkin. Like a beacon on the Texas plains, its retro neon sign lured me in. It's one thing to find an überhip coffee shop in New Orleans or Austin, another thing altogether on this rural side of the Lone Star State. General manager Ben Harbuck sees it as his personal mission to bring exceptional coffee, art, and music to this community. In fact, he pulled me the most exquisite latte I've ever sipped. The inventive drinks menu offers more than a few surprises. If you go, make sure to try the "Black Spot" latte, named for the pirates' mark in Treasure Island.

Standpipe Coffee House Irish Lodge au Lait

Even if you're not a fan of amaretto, you'll like this sweet coffee. Look for the flavored syrups made especially for coffee drinks near the coffee beans in the grocery store.

1   cup 2% reduced-fat milk, steamed
¼   cup freshly brewed espresso
1   Tbsp. Irish cream syrup
1   Tbsp. amaretto syrup
1   Tbsp. toffee syrup
Whipped cream

1. Stir together first 5 ingredients in a large coffee mug; top with whipped cream. **Makes 1 serving.**

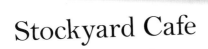

Stockyard Cafe

101 South Manhattan Street
Amarillo, Texas
(806) 342-9411

Horses whinny, a freight train rumbles by, and small clouds of dust swirl up around my boots as I walk into this Amarillo classic. The place is full of real cowboys, who come in from the auction next door or nearby ranches to eat Texas staples such as chicken-fried steak and green chili. They appreciate the fare—and the owner's impressive cooking résumé. "That Tim Youngblood went to culinary school and worked for Donald Trump," one horse trader told me. It's true. Though he now runs a simple cafe, Tim does it with tremendous care, elevating the ordinary to an art form.

Stockyard Cafe Green Chili

Perfect for dinner around a campfire, this hearty stew is not green in color. The green in the name refers to the green chiles in it. Serve it with steamed white rice and grilled corn tortillas.

3¾ lb. boneless pork loin, cut in 1-inch cubes

6 Tbsp. bacon drippings or vegetable oil, divided

2 cups chopped yellow onion

3 Tbsp. New Mexico or Southwestern chipotle powder

2 Tbsp. minced garlic

10 cups chicken broth

2½ cups chopped roasted, seeded green Hatch chiles or 3 (10-oz.) cans seeded green chiles, drained and chopped

1 (10-oz.) can extra spicy diced tomatoes and green chiles

2 baking potatoes, peeled and coarsely chopped (3 cups)

⅔ cup all-purpose flour

Garnish: minced fresh cilantro

1. Brown one-third of pork in 1 tsp. hot bacon drippings in a large skillet over high heat, stirring 5 minutes or until browned on all sides. Remove pork from skillet using a slotted spoon; reserve drippings in skillet. Repeat procedure twice with 2 tsp. bacon drippings and remaining pork.

2. Sauté onion, chipotle powder, and garlic in 1 tsp. hot bacon drippings in a large stockpot over medium-high heat 2 to 3 minutes or until fragrant. Add pork, broth, green chiles, and tomatoes. Bring to a boil; reduce heat, and simmer, uncovered, 30 minutes. Stir in potatoes, and simmer, uncovered, 30 minutes or until meat is very tender.

3. Heat remaining bacon drippings in a skillet over medium heat. Whisk flour into drippings, and cook over medium-low heat, whisking constantly, until mixture is the color of peanut butter, about 10 minutes.

4. Remove 2 cups broth from stockpot; gradually whisk into roux. Gradually stir roux mixture into chili. Bring to a boil, and boil 3 minutes or until thickened and bubbly. **Makes 17½ cups.**

Stockyard Cafe Chicken-Fried Steak

This is truly smothered in gravy and may give you an immediate coronary, but it's worth it. You don't have to partially freeze the steaks, but it helps the breading adhere and yields a crunchier coating.

8   (6-oz.) cubed steaks
Parchment paper
2   cups buttermilk
3   large eggs
1½   cups all-purpose flour
1   tsp. salt
¼   tsp. pepper
6   Tbsp. Clarified Butter (at right) or peanut oil
Country Gravy (at right)
½   cup chopped roasted Hatch chiles or 1 (4-oz.)
     can chopped fire-roasted green chiles

1. Arrange steaks in a single layer on a baking sheet lined with parchment paper. Freeze 30 minutes.
2. Whisk together buttermilk and eggs in a medium bowl. Stir together flour, salt, and pepper in a pie plate or shallow dish. Dip partially frozen steaks in egg mixture; dredge in flour mixture, shaking off excess. Return to baking sheet.
3. Heat 2 Tbsp. Clarified Butter in a large cast-iron skillet over medium-high heat. Add 3 steaks; cook 4 minutes on each side or until steaks are desired degree of doneness and breading is golden brown. Place steaks on a wire rack in a jelly-roll pan, and keep warm in a 200° oven. Repeat procedure two times with remaining Clarified Butter and steaks.
4. To serve, spoon Country Gravy over steaks, and top with green chiles. **Makes 8 servings.**

Clarified Butter

Clarifying removes milk solids from butter, raising its smoke point and allowing longer frying without burning—especially important for chicken-fried dishes. This basic recipe can be doubled, tripled, or multiplied as needed. Note that you lose about one-quarter of the original butter amount during the clarifying process.

½   cup unsalted butter, roughly chopped

1. Melt butter in a saucepan over low heat. Remove from heat when it liquefies and separates into three layers: white foam on top, yellow liquid in the middle, and tiny brown specks at the bottom. (Liquid should not be brown.) Let stand 3 minutes. Skim foam from top with a slotted spoon. Carefully pour yellow liquid into a clean jar or other container, leaving solids in bottom of pan. Discard foam and solids. **Makes 6 Tbsp.**

Country Gravy

4   cups milk
¼   cup bacon drippings or vegetable oil
½   cup all-purpose flour
1   tsp. salt
½   tsp. freshly ground pepper

1. Cook milk in a small heavy saucepan over low heat 15 minutes or until warm.
2. Meanwhile, heat bacon drippings in a heavy skillet over medium heat. Whisk flour into drippings, and cook over medium-low heat, whisking constantly, until mixture is the color of peanut butter (about 10 minutes).
3. Gradually whisk in warm milk; cook over medium heat, whisking constantly, until mixture is thickened and bubbly. Stir in salt and pepper. **Makes 3 cups.**

Stockyard Cafe

Brush up on your swagger before coming here. Try walking bowlegged or blurting, "You mess with the bull, you get the horns." Call random people "hombre." Stuff like that. 'Cause this place is as Texas as it gets. People wear Chevy hubcaps for belt buckles and iron their Wranglers (a capital fashion crime in most places). These are real cattlemen—not some Hollywood version. They've seen things: harsh plains, big storms, the inner workings of a cow's hindquarters. The good news: You don't actually have to see such horrors to be comforted by a giant plate of chicken-fried steak and a heaping bowl of green chili stew.

Nic's Grill

1201 North Pennsylvania Avenue
Oklahoma City, Oklahoma
(405) 524-0999

"I cook the way I like to eat," says Justin "Nic" Nicholas. And a lot of people like to eat the way Nic does. Nic's Grill, which seats a mere 20, is crammed with locals any given day of the week. Why? Start with the half-pound cheeseburger. Topped with onion, cheese, and jalapeños, it's my favorite classic burger. It costs just $4.95, so you can afford to splurge and get house-cut curly fries. Or go for breakfast and indulge in one of Nic's massive omelets. No matter how big your appetite, you'll leave this tiny Oklahoma City diner stuffed and satisfied.

Nic's Western Omelet

At the restaurant, this ginormous omelet is one serving, but it really makes enough to feed two. It's less about the egg than about the big chunks of tasty ingredients inside.

½   cup sliced portobello mushrooms
1   jalapeño pepper, seeded and sliced
Pinch of salt
1   Tbsp. vegetable oil
1   Tbsp. butter
1   cup coarsely chopped ham
½   cup coarsely chopped tomato
½   cup vertically sliced white onion
¼   cup chopped green bell pepper
3   large eggs
Pinch of salt
Pinch of pepper
1   cup (4 oz.) shredded sharp Cheddar cheese

1. Sauté mushrooms, jalapeño pepper, and pinch of salt in hot oil in a large nonstick skillet over medium-high heat 5 minutes or until mushrooms release their juices and brown. Transfer mixture to a bowl. Wipe skillet clean with paper towels.
2. Melt butter in skillet over medium heat. Add ham, tomato, onion, and bell pepper; cook 6 minutes, stirring occasionally. Add ham mixture to mushroom mixture in bowl. Wipe skillet clean with paper towels.
3. Place skillet over medium-high heat. Whisk together eggs, pinch of salt, and pinch of pepper in a medium bowl. Pour eggs into skillet. As egg mixture starts to cook, gently lift edges of omelet with a spatula, and tilt pan so uncooked portion flows underneath. Cook 1 to 2 minutes or until almost set. Sprinkle cheese and ham mixture over omelet. Fold sides of omelet over filling with a spatula, and turn out, seam side down, onto a plate. **Makes 1 to 2 servings.**

OVERHEARD: "Better not to whack a hornet's nest with a short stick."

My Oklahoma City friend Jim is not a man to take unnecessary chances, and this is one of the better tips he gave me when I considered driving my 1955 Cadillac Fleetwood across his home state. It was his nice way of saying, "Don't be a fool."

Nic's Classic Burger

Bet you can't put down this gooey two-handed job!

2   lb. ground chuck
1   tsp. salt
½   tsp. freshly ground pepper
1½ Tbsp. vegetable oil, divided
1   large white onion, thinly sliced
4   jalapeño peppers, thinly sliced
Pinch of salt
8   (1-oz.) processed American cheese slices
4   hamburger buns
3   Tbsp. mayonnaise
3   Tbsp. yellow mustard
1   cup shredded lettuce
2   ripe tomatoes, cut into ¼-inch-thick slices

1. Shape ground beef into 4 (½-inch-thick) patties; sprinkle with 1 tsp. salt and pepper.
2. Cook patties in 1½ tsp. hot oil in a large cast-iron skillet over medium heat about 7 minutes on each side for medium-well, or 9 minutes on each side for well-done.
3. While burgers cook, sauté onion, jalapeño peppers, and pinch of salt in 1 Tbsp. hot oil in a medium skillet over medium-high heat 12 minutes or until onions are browned.
4. During the last minute of the burgers' cook time, place 2 cheese slices on each patty; cover with lid. Remove skillet from heat; let stand, covered, to melt cheese.
5. Preheat broiler with oven rack 3 inches from heat. Place buns, cut sides up, on a baking sheet. Broil 1 minute or until lightly toasted.
6. Spread mayonnaise on bottom halves of buns; spread mustard on top halves of buns. Layer lettuce, tomato slices, cheese-topped patty, and onion-pepper mixture in buns. Serve with a knife and lots of paper towels. **Makes 4 servings.**

Nic's Grill

Nic is unaware of America's ongoing cholesterol problem. This knowledge has completely passed him by. I think Nic's must be how people ate in the last ice age. "Hey, Sasquatch, knock that woolly mammoth in the head, and let's eat him. All of him. Ug!" The only difference is now we get a bun and some fries too. And this is why I love Nic's. Shoot, this is why everyone in this town loves Nic's. It's awesomely bad for you but so tremendously good. The best part? Meals here are a serious bargain. If you spend more than $20, you are either buying lunch for three people or have some weird bovine stomach system.

Oklahoma

Rock Cafe

114 West Main Street
Stroud, Oklahoma
(918) 968-3990

Icons abound along America's mother road, Route 66, but few are as steeped in the spirit of adventure as the Rock Cafe, which is back in full force despite a fire nearly destroying it in 2008. The cafe is situated in tiny Stroud, Oklahoma, where the Southwest, the Midwest, and the Southeast seem to collide. Consequently, you'll find everything from delicious fry bread to peach cobbler on its menu. Even better are owner Dawn Welch's stories. Her enthusiasm for America and those who travel its scenic byways inspired the Sally character in Pixar's Cars. Dawn collects friends like some chefs collect recipes. Her welcoming spirit helps put the kick in Route 66.

Rock Cafe
Indian Fry-Bread Tacos

These open-faced beauties are simple and delicious.

3½ cups self-rising flour, divided
½   cup sugar
1½ cups very warm water (not lukewarm, not hot)
4   cups vegetable oil, divided
8   cups chili (such as Hillbilly Chili, page 98), warmed
Toppings: shredded cheese, shredded lettuce, chopped green onions, chopped tomato, sour cream

1. Stir together 2½ cups flour and sugar in a large bowl. Add warm water, stirring until a batter forms. Cover with a clean cloth, and let rise in a warm place (85°), free from drafts, 30 minutes or until slightly puffy and evenly moistened.
2. Spread remaining 1 cup flour in a thick layer on a work surface. Using a rubber spatula, turn dough out onto floured work surface. Flour hands liberally, turn them palms up, and slip them under the dough. Fold edges over onto the dough several times until a soft, yet cohesive, dough forms (it will be slightly lumpy with some floury streaks). Knead dough 3 or 4 times until it forms a ball.
3. Grease a large bowl with ½ tsp. oil; place dough in bowl, turning to grease top. Cover with a clean towel, and let rise in a warm place (85°), free from drafts, 30 minutes or until puffy.
4. Divide dough into 8 equal portions. Pat each portion of dough into a 5- to 6-inch circle. Make hole in center of circle using your finger on a floured surface with floured hands.
5. Pour remaining oil into a 3-qt. saucepan; heat to 350°. Fry dough circles, 1 at a time, 2 minutes on each side or until lightly browned. Drain on paper towels. To serve, place fry bread on individual plates. Top each with 1 cup chili and desired toppings. **Makes 8 servings.**

Rock Cafe Easy Peach Cobbler

This simple cobbler—made with ingredients you probably already have on hand—is an Oklahoma classic. Serve with vanilla ice cream for a more decadent dessert.

- 1 cup all-purpose flour
- ¾ cup sugar
- ½ tsp. baking powder
- ½ cup cold butter, cut up
- 2 (15-oz.) cans sliced peaches in light syrup, drained

1. Preheat oven to 375°. Whisk together flour, sugar, and baking powder in a medium bowl; cut in butter with a pastry blender or two forks until mixture forms pea- to blueberry-size pieces.

2. Place peaches in a lightly greased 8-inch square baking dish. Sprinkle flour mixture over peaches.

3. Bake at 375° for 45 to 50 minutes or until bubbly and golden brown. Let stand 15 minutes before serving. **Makes 6 servings.**

SOUNDTRACK:

"Blown Away" by Muskogee native Carrie Underwood

"I Like Girls That Drink Beer" by Clinton native Toby Keith

"You're Driving Me Crazy (What Did I Do)" by Chet Baker

"Consider Me Gone" by McAlester native Reba McEntire

"The Thunder Rolls" by Yukon native Garth Brooks

"The End" by the Kings of Leon

GUEST CHECK

Date — Table — Guests — Server
Sweet 10 130766

APPT—SOUP/SAL—ENTREE—VEG/POT—DESSERT—BEV

3 cups mashd sw pot.
1 cup sugar
1 stick oleo
2 eggs beaten
1 T. vanilla

Topping:
1 c. Br. sugar
1/3 cup oleo
1/3 cup flour
1 cup nuts

Sweet potato

Tax
Total

3632   www.nationalchecking.com

Abigail's

206 Central Street
Rocheport, Missouri
(573) 698-3000

In the tiny town of Rocheport, population 239, not much changes. The sleepy streets, quaint post office, and meandering river still look the same as they did when I first visited more than a decade ago. Likewise, Abigail's continues to consistently delight diners with dishes such as lemon-pecan linguine and toffee nut pie. Tourists from around the world find their way to this whimsical restaurant, and many keep coming back. Pull off the highway (or pedal off the Katy Trail) to try Abigail's, and you'll understand why.

Abigail's Sweet Lemon-Pecan Linguine

Sweet and tart, this is a best-seller at Abigail's. The restaurant offers it as a stand-alone dish, with optional toppings such as sliced grilled chicken or grilled shrimp.

¾   cup pecan halves
1   (16-oz.) package uncooked linguine
½   cup butter
4   garlic cloves, minced
¼   tsp. salt
¼   tsp. freshly ground pepper
½   cup sugar
½   cup fresh lemon juice
⅓   cup dry white wine
1   cup freshly grated Parmigiano-Reggiano cheese
     or Asiago cheese
Garnish: lemon zest

1. Preheat oven to 350°. Bake pecans in a single layer in a shallow pan 6 to 8 minutes or until toasted and fragrant, stirring halfway through. Roughly chop ¼ cup pecans.

2. Cook pasta in a large Dutch oven according to package directions; drain, reserving ¾ cup cooking water. Rinse pasta with cool water; drain well, and return pasta to Dutch oven.

3. Melt butter in a large skillet over medium heat; add garlic, and sauté 1 minute. Add chopped pecans, salt, and pepper; sauté 1 minute. Add sugar and lemon juice, and cook, stirring constantly, until sugar dissolves. Continue cooking until mixture slightly thickens, about 2 minutes. Stir in reserved ¾ cup pasta cooking water and wine; pour sauce over pasta in Dutch oven, tossing to coat.

4. Cook pasta mixture, stirring constantly, over medium-high heat 1 to 2 minutes or until thoroughly heated. Spoon into bowls; top with remaining pecan halves and cheese. **Makes 4 servings.**

OVERHEARD: "Who's pluckin' this chicken—me or you?"

I often want to use this Missouri expression when I'm "discussing" what restaurants to visit with friends. Usually, I find I ain't pluckin' the chicken after all.

Abigail's Toffee Nut Pie

This is what you'd get if a pecan pie and a Heath bar had a love child.

⅔   cup chopped pecans
⅔   cup chopped natural almonds
¼   cup butter
½   cup sugar
3   large eggs
1   cup light corn syrup
½   (14.1-oz.) package refrigerated piecrusts
¾   cup toffee bits
Garnishes: whipped cream, toffee bits, chopped nuts

1. Preheat oven to 350°. Bake pecans and almonds at 350° in a single layer in a shallow pan 8 to 10 minutes or until lightly toasted and fragrant, stirring halfway through.
2. Beat butter and sugar at high speed with an electric mixer until light and fluffy. Add eggs, 1 at a time, beating well after each addition. Add corn syrup, beating until blended.
3. Fit piecrust into a 9-inch pie plate according to package directions; fold edges under, and crimp. Pour corn syrup mixture into piecrust. Sprinkle with toasted nuts and toffee bits. Bake at 350° for 40 minutes or until set. Remove from oven to a wire rack, and cool completely (about 2 hours). **Makes 8 servings.**

Abigail's

Let's say you and your beloved are staying in the vineyards and pedaling Missouri's acclaimed Katy Trail, the biking paradise reclaimed from old railroad lines. Exercise and fresh air sounded great, and the pictures of Schwinning couples looked oh-so-fabulous. Never mind that you haven't been on a bike since second grade and are now sweating like a sinner at an August tent revival as you try to pedal to Rocheport. (Gee, that picture isn't on bikekatytrail.com!) So, how you gonna salvage this vacation? Eat at Abigail's. Delicious dishes such as sweet lemon pecan pasta and toffee nut pie will restore any good humor you lost while exercising like some grammar-school kid. Then you can kick back for hours, drinking wine, and swapping bike-trail survival stories.

Vintage Restaurant Sausage Strudel Pie

2 medium baking potatoes, diced
2 lb. ground pork sausage
2 cups drained jarred refrigerated sauerkraut
1 cup chopped fresh mushrooms
1 Tbsp. caraway seeds
½ tsp. salt
½ tsp. freshly ground pepper
½ cup butter, melted
12 frozen phyllo sheets, thawed
Sour cream
Garnish: dill sprigs

1. Cook potatoes in boiling salted water to cover 10 minutes or until tender; drain. Meanwhile, brown sausage in a large skillet over medium-high heat, stirring often, 15 minutes or until sausage crumbles and is no longer pink; drain and return to skillet. Let cool 15 minutes. Stir in potatoes, sauerkraut, and next 4 ingredients.

2. Preheat oven to 375°. Brush 6 (1½-cup) gratin dishes with melted butter. Center 2 phyllo sheets over 1 buttered gratin dish. (Phyllo will hang over edge of gratin dishes. Keep remaining phyllo covered with a damp towel to prevent drying out.) Spoon 1½ cups sausage mixture onto phyllo in dish; fold overhanging phyllo dough over filling to cover, and crimp. Brush phyllo with melted butter. Repeat with remaining phyllo, sausage mixture, and butter.

3. Place gratin dishes on a jelly-roll pan. Bake at 375° for 12 to 15 minutes or until golden brown. Serve with sour cream. **Makes 6 servings.**

Note: We tested with Bubbies Old Fashioned Sauerkraut, found in the refrigerated section.

Vintage Restaurant at Stone Hill Winery

1110 Stone Hill Highway
Hermann, Missouri
(573) 486-3479

I'm eating in a barn. In fact, hay was once dropped down from the loft above to a trough next to my table. Nearly everything at Stone Hill Winery boasts a fascinating history. Its most celebrated wine, the Norton, is made from a native local grape. The delicious and complex red pairs beautifully with the restaurant's spaetzle and its sausage strudel pie. If the menu sounds a little Germanic, that's because we're in Hermann, where it's not unusual to see men in lederhosen. Explore the town, take a vineyard tour, buy a souvenir case of Stone Hill's award-winning wines, have dinner at the Vintage, and you'll be saying, "Gott sei Dank für Speis' und Trank!" just like a local.

Vintage Restaurant Spaetzle

Spaetzle (SHPAYTZ-lah) are a cross between dumplings and noodles. This hearty dish, with a sausage and mushroom sauce, is anything but bland.

Sauce

1	lb. ground pork sausage
1	cup chopped fresh mushrooms
1	cup chopped onion
½	cup diced red bell pepper
⅛	tsp. salt
⅛	tsp. pepper
2	cups heavy cream
1	cup crumbled blue cheese

Spaetzle

4	cups all-purpose flour
1½	tsp. salt
1	tsp. ground nutmeg
½	tsp. ground white pepper
8	large eggs
1	cup milk

1. Prepare Sauce: Brown sausage in a large skillet over medium-high heat, stirring often, 10 minutes or until sausage crumbles and is no longer pink. Remove sausage from skillet using a slotted spoon; reserve 1½ Tbsp. drippings in skillet.

2. Sauté mushrooms and next 4 ingredients in drippings in skillet over medium-high heat 7 minutes or until vegetables are tender. Stir in sausage and cream; bring to a boil. Reduce heat, and simmer, stirring often, 6 minutes or until thickened. Remove from heat; stir in blue cheese. Keep warm.

3. Prepare Spaetzle: Whisk together flour and next 3 ingredients in a large bowl; make a well in center of mixture. Whisk eggs in another large bowl. Whisk in milk; add to dry mixture, stirring until moistened.

4. Bring a large stockpot half-full of salted water to a boil; place a large-holed metal colander on top of stockpot (colander should not touch water). Press half of dough through holes of colander into the boiling water using the back of a spoon. Cook 1 minute or until spaetzle float. Remove spaetzle with a slotted spoon or mesh spider; keep warm. Repeat procedure with remaining dough. Toss spaetzle with sauce. **Makes 6 servings.**

Godsey's Grill ↙

J.D. Maggard's STORE

Boulevard Bread Company ↙

Little Rock

Jonesboro

Stinky & Coco's
1 North Main St.
Winchester, KY 40391
(859) 744-8100
www.stinkyandcocos.com

The Family Wash ↓

Nashville

Uncle Lou's Fried Chicken ↙

Memphis

Tennessee

GOOD DOG

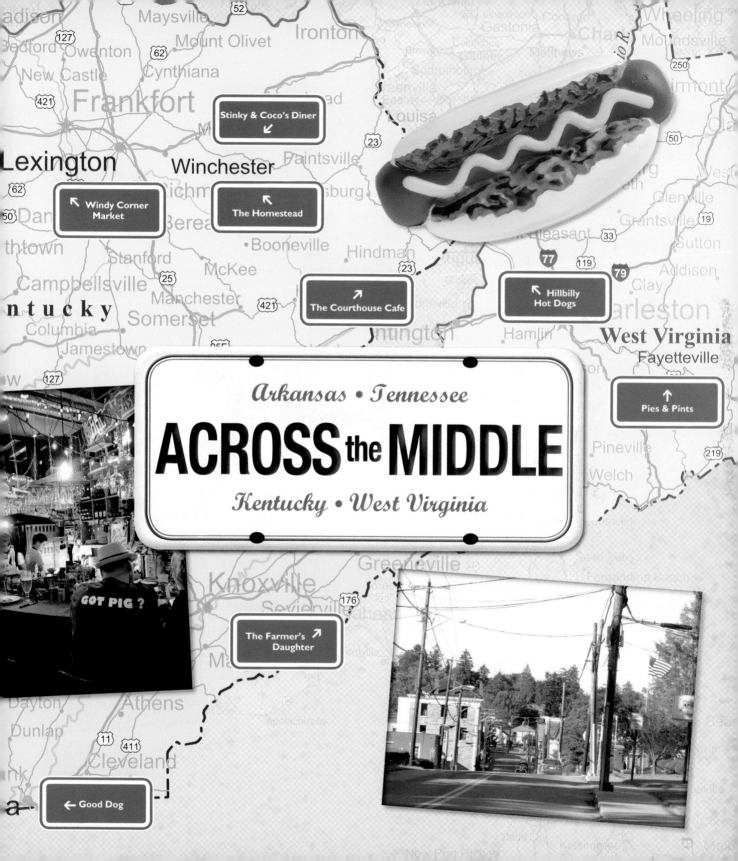

Stinky & Coco's Diner

Windy Corner Market

The Homestead

The Courthouse Cafe

Hillbilly Hot Dogs

Pies & Pints

GOT PIG ?

Arkansas • Tennessee

ACROSS the MIDDLE

Kentucky • West Virginia

The Farmer's Daughter

Good Dog

ANP BABY
ROMA TOMATOES
$5.00
CONTAINER

Boulevard Bread Company

1920 North Grant Street
Little Rock, Arkansas
(501) 663-5951

Perfect cappuccinos, healthy salads, decadent cheeses, and the smell of freshly baked bread make Boulevard Bread Company my favorite destination in Little Rock. Its counters brim with local produce and gourmet chocolates you'll want to savor. They're unabashed coffee snobs here: Perfectly pulled shots of espresso will put a kick in your step on the way to the capitol. Owners Christina Basham and Sonia Schaefer adore tomatoes as much as I do, so don't miss their Tomato Tapenade, a phenomenal appetizer that can be whipped up well in advance, or the delightful tomato-and-bread salad known as panzanella. And don't forget to save room for their incredible lemon cookies.

Boulevard Cucumber-Quinoa Salad

This refreshing side salad is a great accompaniment to grilled meats and a good way to pack some whole grains into your Southern road trip.

1   (12-oz.) package quinoa
3   cups halved heirloom cherry tomatoes
2   cups peeled, seeded, and diced cucumber
¼   cup diced red onion
¼   cup thinly sliced fresh mint
1   Tbsp. minced fresh oregano
½   cup olive oil
¼   cup fresh lemon juice
1   Tbsp. kosher salt
1   tsp. freshly ground pepper
Garnish: fresh mint

1. Cook quinoa according to package directions. Spread out on a jelly-roll pan, and cool completely (about 20 minutes).
2. Toss together quinoa, tomatoes, and next 4 ingredients in a large bowl. Whisk together oil, lemon juice, salt, and pepper in a small bowl; drizzle over salad, and toss. Cover and chill 2 to 8 hours to let flavors combine. **Makes 8 servings.**

Boulevard Tomato Tapenade

Don't discard the flavorful juice from the tomatoes.
Save it for soup or a fresh Bloody Mary.

1½ cups dry white wine

1 cup sun-dried tomatoes, cut into strips

1 (28-oz.) can whole San Marzano or other plum tomatoes, drained and chopped

½ cup diced Vidalia onion

1 large garlic clove, sliced

½ cup olive oil, divided

½ cup drained and rinsed capers

¼ cup chopped fresh parsley

¾ tsp. salt

Toasted French baguette slices

1. Bring first 3 ingredients to a boil in a medium saucepan over high heat. Reduce heat, and simmer 45 minutes, stirring every 10 minutes, until thickened. Cool completely (about 20 minutes).
2. Sauté onion and garlic in ½ tsp. hot oil in a medium skillet over medium-high heat 4 minutes.
3. Stir onion mixture, remaining oil, capers, parsley, and salt into tomato mixture. Serve immediately with toasted French baguette slices, or cover and chill up to 3 days. Serve at room temperature. **Makes 2½ cups.**

Boulevard Panzanella

Toss this bread salad together just before serving so the toasted croutons just begin to soak up the tomato juices and dressing.

1 medium shallot, thinly sliced

1 Tbsp. red wine vinegar

½ (16-oz.) loaf sourdough bread (or any crusty European-style bread), cut into bite-size pieces

3 Tbsp. extra virgin olive oil

1½ Tbsp. balsamic vinegar

½ tsp. salt

¼ tsp. freshly ground pepper

3 heirloom tomatoes, cut in bite-size pieces (5 cups)

2 cups halved heirloom cherry tomatoes

½ cup loosely packed basil leaves, thinly sliced

1. Preheat oven to 400°. Toss together shallot and red wine vinegar in a large bowl; let stand 15 minutes.
2. Place bread in a single layer on a baking sheet, and bake at 400° for 5 minutes or until crisp and lightly browned, stirring occasionally.
3. Stir olive oil, balsamic vinegar, salt, and pepper into shallot mixture. Add croutons, tomatoes, and basil; toss gently to coat. Serve immediately.
Makes 4 servings.

SOUNDTRACK:

"L-O-V-E" by Arkansas native Al Green

"Arkansas Traveler" by Byron Berline

"Stage Fright" by The Band

"Folsom Prison Blues" by Arkansas native Johnny Cash

"Jim Dandy" by Black Oak Arkansas

"Born to Wander" by The Cate Brothers

"Arkansas" from the musical Big River

Boulevard Lemon Cookies

These fluffy lemon cookies, a recipe I begged for, lash the tongue with sweet-tart goodness. Good luck eating just one.

2   cups sugar
1   cup unsalted butter, softened
½   tsp. lemon zest
2   large eggs
1½ tsp. vanilla extract
1   tsp. lemon oil
4   cups all-purpose flour
1½ tsp. baking soda
½   tsp. salt
½   cup fresh lemon juice
1   cup powdered sugar

1. Preheat oven to 350°. Beat sugar, butter, and lemon zest at medium speed with an electric mixer until light and fluffy. Add eggs, vanilla, and lemon oil; beat at low speed until blended. Sift together flour, baking soda, and salt; add to butter mixture alternately with lemon juice, beginning and ending with flour mixture.
2. Scoop dough by tablespoonfuls, and shape into balls; roll in powdered sugar. Place cookies 2 inches apart on lightly greased baking sheets.
3. Bake at 350° for 16 to 18 minutes or just until cookies begin to brown (cookies should be soft in the middle). Cool on baking sheets 2 minutes. Transfer to wire racks. **Makes 4 dozen.**

Boulevard Bread Company

So, I'm standing in this quaint little bakery, minding my own business, when suddenly I hear: "SheshusMaryandJoseph in a Cadillac, that's GOOD!" Everyone in the restaurant turns to stare at the shouter, who is tearing into a lemon cookie as if he were the Cookie Monster, mouth full, crumbs flying, eyes googling around wildly. Yeah, OK, it was me. The cookies, bread, salads, and cheese here kinda make me lose my cool. But Boulevard Bread Company doesn't judge—much.

Godsey's Grill

226 South Main Street
Jonesboro, Arkansas
(870) 336-1988

When it comes to towns with cool night-life, tiny Jonesboro may not spring immediately to mind. Yet this college and farming town boasts a gem in the form of Godsey's Grill, a surprise on Jonesboro's main drag. More than just a pretty face, Godsey's also has some serious personality on its menu. Known for amazing burgers, the popular eatery also roasts up chicken, hickory-smoked barbecue, and pizzas in the city's only wood-fired oven. You won't leave hungry.

Godsey's Kickin' Chicken Sandwiches

Spicy, smoky, and a little sweet, this pulled chicken sandwich delivers. At the restaurant, it's made with meat from whole Cajun-spiced chickens that are slowly smoked over hickory. We made it faster with hot cooked chicken from the grocery deli.

4   pretzel buns or kaiser rolls
Cobra Sauce (below)
¾   lb. pulled smoked or deli-roasted chicken
12   cooked bacon slices
1   large ripe tomato, cut into 8 slices
8   (0.7-oz.) pepper Jack cheese slices

1. Preheat broiler. Split buns, and place, cut sides up, on baking sheet. Broil 6 inches from heat 1 minute or until toasted. Spread cut sides of buns with Cobra Sauce. Set top halves aside. Pile chicken, bacon, tomato, and cheese onto bottom halves of buns. Return to oven, and broil 6 inches from heat 1 minute or until cheese melts. Replace top halves of buns. **Makes 4 servings.**

Cobra Sauce

You can use less Sriracha. But, like its namesake, this rémoulade-like sauce should have some bite.

½   cup mayonnaise
¼   cup ketchup
¼   cup Asian Sriracha hot chili sauce
1   Tbsp. dill pickle juice
½   tsp. granulated garlic
¼   tsp. salt
¼   tsp. freshly ground pepper

1. Stir together all ingredients in a small bowl. **Makes about 1 cup.**

OVERHEARD: "Give me some sugar!"

When someone says this in the South, it doesn't mean pass the Dixie Crystals. It's used when the asker wants a hug, a kiss, or both. Caution: Small nephews may be terrified when this is uttered by large aunts on major holidays.

The Family Wash

2038 Greenwood Avenue
Nashville, Tennessee
(615) 226-6070

On the trendy east side of Nashville, just a few miles from the honky-tonks, sits this former laundry. The Family Wash no longer cleans clothes, but it does spin some outstanding tunes. The funky spot hosts many local bands and remains one of the most intimate places in the Music City to catch a live performance. Don't miss out on the serious comfort food served up here. I'm a fan of what the Brits call pub food, and The Family Wash does it right. The shepherd's pie is one of the best I've had outside of J.O.E. (jolly old England), and the mac-and-cheese has just the right amount of crunchy crust. Both are best devoured with a pint of your favorite ale.

Family Wash Mac & Cheese

This homey mac is gooey without being runny and has a nice crust of browned Cheddar on top. Buy a 1-pound chunk of white American cheese from the deli, and cube it for the sauce. The less expensive the cheese, the better it melts.

1	cup milk
1	lb. processed white American cheese, cubed
2	cups (8 oz.) shredded Cheddar cheese, divided
¾	cup grated Parmesan cheese, divided
1	tsp. salt
1	lb. penne pasta

1. Preheat oven to 450°. Bring milk to a simmer in a large saucepan (do not boil). Add white American cheese, 1 cup Cheddar cheese, ½ cup Parmesan cheese, and salt; cook, stirring constantly, 5 minutes or until cheese melts and sauce is smooth.
2. Meanwhile, cook pasta according to package directions; drain and return to pan. Pour cheese sauce over pasta, tossing to coat.
3. Pour mixture into a lightly greased 11- x 7-inch baking dish. Sprinkle with remaining 1 cup Cheddar cheese and ¼ cup Parmesan cheese. Bake at 450° for 15 minutes or until Cheddar cheese is melted and golden brown. **Makes 8 servings.**

Family Wash Shepherd's Pie

Dense, delicious, and beefy, this dish is served very hot.

Filling

1	lb. ground round
½	lb. ground lamb
1¼	cups fresh or frozen green peas
1	cup diced carrot
1	cup diced yellow onion
1	cup stout beer
1½	Tbsp. dried basil
1½	Tbsp. dried oregano
1	Tbsp. dried thyme
1½	tsp. kosher salt
1	tsp. ground white pepper

Topping

2	lb. large Yukon gold potatoes, peeled and quartered
1¾	tsp. kosher salt, divided
½	cup heavy cream
3	Tbsp. butter
3	cups (12 oz.) shredded white Cheddar cheese

1. Prepare Filling: Brown ground beef and lamb in a large skillet over medium-high heat, stirring often, 10 to 12 minutes or until meat crumbles and is no longer pink. Add peas and next 8 ingredients; bring to a boil. Reduce heat, and simmer, uncovered, 8 minutes or until vegetables are tender.

2. Prepare Topping: Bring potatoes, ¾ tsp. salt, and water to cover to a boil in a large saucepan over high heat. Reduce heat, and simmer, uncovered, 15 to 20 minutes or until tender. Drain and return to pan. Add cream, butter, and remaining 1 tsp. salt; mash with a wooden spoon or potato masher until no large lumps remain.

3. Preheat oven to 450°. Spoon 1 cup Filling into each of 6 lightly greased (2-cup) baking dishes. Top each serving with about 1 cup Topping, spreading to edges. Sprinkle each pie with ½ cup cheese, and bake at 450° for 20 minutes or until cheese is golden. **Makes 6 servings.**

Note: We tested with Guinness for the stout beer.

OVERHEARD: "If I were doing any better, I'd have to take worse pills!"

When I was stationed in Afghanistan, one of my Navy chiefs (who was from Knoxville) used to say this whenever I asked how he was doing. It never ceased to make me smile, even in a place where we weren't doing much smiling.

The Farmer's Daughter

**7700 Erwin Highway
Chuckey, Tennessee
(423) 257-4650**

It's in a field. It's open only on Fridays, Saturdays, and Sundays. Pretty girls in blue gingham dash hither and yon with piled-high platters of Southern staples: ripe water-melon, mashed potatoes, and fried green tomatoes. Owners Dan and Rachel Tyson never stray far from their beloved week-end restaurant. Dan met Rachel, an actual farmer's daughter, while returning a melon to her father's produce stand. Years later, the couple's attention to detail and the weekend-on-the-farm setting keep this res-taurant a cut above. Rachel says, "There's no beach that can compare to being here at 5 o'clock on a Saturday night with a band playing and children running around out front." I couldn't agree more.

Farmer's Daughter Biscuits

These fluffy little gems have a savory quality and melt in your mouth—likely (on both accounts) owing to lard and good buttermilk. Your hands may smell a little porky after kneading the dough. But my, oh my, are these biscuits good.

2   cups self-rising soft-wheat flour
½   cup cold lard, cut up
1   cup buttermilk

1. Freeze flour in a large bowl for 30 minutes before making dough. Preheat oven to 450°.
2. Cut lard into cold flour with a pastry blender or fork until crumbly. (Do not overwork.) Add buttermilk, and work it in with your fingers just until dry ingredients are moistened.
3. Turn dough out onto a lightly floured surface, and knead 3 or 4 times. Pat or roll dough to ½-inch thickness; cut with a 1½-inch round cutter dipped in flour. (Do not twist cutter; just push straight down.) Place biscuits on a lightly greased baking sheet.
4. Bake at 450° for 10 to 12 minutes or until golden brown. **Makes 2½ dozen.**

Farmer's Daughter Skillet Cornbread

This is very rich and moist. Even Yankees who don't care for cornbread are bound to like this version.

1½ cups stone-ground white cornmeal
½ cup all-purpose soft-wheat flour
1½ tsp. baking powder
1½ tsp. kosher salt
1½ cups buttermilk
5 Tbsp. unsalted butter, melted and divided
1 large egg

1. Preheat oven to 400°. Heat a 9-inch cast-iron skillet in oven 10 minutes.
2. Stir together cornmeal, flour, baking powder, and salt in a medium bowl. Whisk together buttermilk, half of butter, and egg; add to flour mixture, stirring just until dry ingredients are moistened.
3. Pour remaining half of melted butter into hot skillet; pour batter into skillet. Bake at 400° for 25 minutes or until golden brown and cornbread pulls away from sides of skillet. **Makes 8 servings.**

Note: The Tysons insist the secret here is stone-ground cornmeal. They get theirs from Linney's Mill in Union Grove, North Carolina.

SOUNDTRACK:

"Sequestered in Memphis" by The Hold Steady

"Staring at the Sun" by Jason Aldean

"What Was I Thinking" by Dierks Bentley

"Lovin' You Is Fun" by Easton Corbin

"Mud on the Tires" by Brad Paisley

Farmer's Daughter Bacon and Okra Skillet

This scrumptious dish makes a perfect partner for grilled chicken or fish.

6   slices bacon
2   cups chopped onions
2   cups sliced (¼-inch) okra
2   cups diced tomatoes
½   tsp. salt
½   tsp. freshly ground pepper
3   cups cooked white rice

1. Fry bacon in a 12-inch cast-iron skillet until crisp. Remove and drain on paper towels, reserving drippings in skillet. Add onions and okra to skillet, and cook over medium heat, stirring occasionally, until tender, 7 to 10 minutes. Add diced tomatoes, and cook 7 minutes more. Season with salt and pepper. Crumble bacon on top. Serve with rice. **Makes 4 to 6 servings.**

The Farmer's Daughter

When you go here, you're going to be all: "That Morgan Murphy is a genius! How does he find these places, so full of optimism, sunshine, and unbelievable food, and with staffs that are so friendly and welcoming?" Yeah, just like that. The Farmer's Daughter is so fine you'll want to throw me a parade (with floats) or be the president of my cheerleading squad. I'm *that* confident you'll love this place as much as I do. They do things right. Take the cornbread for instance. It's buttery and warm and practically begging to be sopped in gravy. You could stop right there and the cornbread would be enough. You'd eat it and be blissfully happy. (That parade? I'd like it on my birthday, thanks.)

Tennessee

Good Dog

34 Frazier Avenue
Chattanooga, Tennessee
(423) 475-6175

At the ballpark, at a backyard cookout, and even from the corner "dirty-water dog" cart—sometimes you just want a hot dog. When in Chattanooga, I head to Good Dog, whose gourmet, all-beef, naturally cased dogs defy description. At her kitschy spot just across the river from the Chattanooga Aquarium, Susan Paden offers up a dizzying array of flavor combinations. To make them at home, Susan suggests starting with a toasted, fresh, local bun. Smear one side with brown mustard and the other with cream cheese. Add a grilled all-beef dog. Top it with Onion Sauce or Curry Ketchup, and you've got yourself one good dog, for sure.

Good Dog Ketchup

This has an excellent flavor and isn't too sweet. Double it to make both the Onion Sauce and Curry Ketchup.

- 1   (6-oz.) can tomato paste
- ½   cup honey
- ½   cup white vinegar
- 1   tsp. salt
- ½   tsp. onion powder
- ½   tsp. garlic powder

1. Whisk together ¼ cup water, tomato paste, and remaining ingredients in a medium saucepan. Bring to a boil over medium heat; reduce heat, and simmer, stirring often, 30 minutes or until slightly thickened. Remove from heat, and cool completely (about 1½ hours). Cover and store in refrigerator up to 3 weeks. **Makes 1½ cups.**

Good Dog Onion Sauce

Sweet and slightly spicy, this sauce jazzes up the ordinary dog.

- 4   cups sliced yellow onion (2 medium)
- 1   Tbsp. olive oil
- 1½   cups Good Dog Ketchup (above) or ready-made ketchup if you're short on time
- ½   tsp. hot sauce
- ⅛   tsp. salt
- ⅛   tsp. ground cinnamon
- ⅛   tsp. chili powder

1. Sauté onions in hot oil in a large saucepan over medium-high heat 5 minutes or until softened. Stir in ½ cup water, ketchup, and remaining ingredients. Bring to a boil; reduce heat, and simmer, stirring constantly, 20 minutes or until thickened. Store in refrigerator up to 3 weeks. **Makes 2½ cups.**

Good Dog Curry Ketchup

*Call it ketchup with a kick and try it as a dip,
on a hot dog, or with bratwurst.*

½   small yellow onion
1½ cups Good Dog Ketchup (at left) or ready-
      made ketchup, if you're short on time
1½ tsp. curry powder

1. Process onion in a food processor 20 seconds
or until smooth. Add ketchup and curry powder;
process 20 seconds or until well blended. Cover
and store in refrigerator up to 3 weeks.
Makes 1½ cups.

Uncle Lou's Southern Kitchen

3633 Millbranch Road
Memphis, Tennessee
(901) 332-2367

Mere blocks from Graceland, Louis "Uncle Lou" Martin III serves up some fixin's Elvis surely would love. Fried baloney sandwiches, "Monster Burgers," deep-fried creamed-corn nuggets, and honey-butter biscuits fill the menu of his unassuming storefront. But it's his Grandmother Medea's recipe for fried chicken that brings in visitors from around the world. This stuff is crazy juicy, crispy, sweet, and spicy. Go there. Have some. Right now. If you can't get to Memphis or aren't able to save room for dessert while you're there, try the restaurant's signature icings on your favorite cake. Bet they'll have you all shook up.

Uncle Lou's Caramel Icing

As caramel icings go, this far-from-ornery one is decidedly easy to prepare.

1¾ cups powdered sugar
½   cup salted butter
½   cup unsalted butter
1   cup firmly packed light brown sugar
6   Tbsp. heavy cream
1½ tsp. vanilla extract

1. Place powdered sugar in a large bowl. Melt salted and unsalted butter in a small saucepan over low heat. Add brown sugar and cream, whisking until all lumps are dissolved. Bring to a boil over medium heat. Remove from heat; stir in vanilla.
2. Pour hot butter-cream mixture into powdered sugar; beat at high speed with an electric mixer 2 minutes or until blended. Cool 1 hour, stirring occasionally. **Makes 2½ cups.**

Uncle Lou's Chocolate Icing

Very sweet, very creamy, and a little thinner than most, this icing is ideal for a 13- x 9-inch cake.

3   oz. cream cheese, softened
2   Tbsp. butter, softened
1   lb. powdered sugar
⅓   cup unsweetened cocoa
½   cup evaporated milk
½   tsp. vanilla extract

1. Beat cream cheese and butter at high speed with an electric mixer until smooth. Whisk together powdered sugar and cocoa; add to cream cheese mixture alternately with evaporated milk, beginning and ending with powdered sugar mixture. Beat at low speed just until blended after each addition. Add vanilla, beating just until blended. **Makes 2⅝ cups.**

Courthouse Cafe Hot Turkey Salad

Think of this as a hot variant of chicken salad. The restaurant serves it on a plate with slices of oven-broiled tomato.

¼ cup chopped walnuts
3 cups diced cooked turkey breast
1 cup (4 oz.) shredded Cheddar cheese
½ cup soft, fresh French bread baguette breadcrumbs
¼ cup chopped celery
¼ cup mayonnaise
¼ tsp. salt

1. Preheat oven to 350°. Bake walnuts in a single layer in an ovenproof pan 5 minutes or until lightly toasted and fragrant, stirring halfway through. Stir together walnuts, turkey, and remaining ingredients in a medium bowl.
2. Spoon mixture into a lightly greased 8-inch square baking dish. Bake at 350° for 25 minutes or until thoroughly heated. **Makes 4 servings.**

The Courthouse Cafe

127 Main Street
Whitesburg, Kentucky
(606) 633-5859

My GPS device sent me in circles looking for the Courthouse Cafe's address in tiny Whitesburg. No doubt about it, when you're in the hills and hollows of eastern Kentucky, friend, you are definitely off the eaten path. Not to worry: Owners Laura Schuster and Josephine and Bill Richardson shrewdly named their restaurant for (and placed it across from) the biggest draw in this city of 1,466: the county courthouse. The food also goes off-map. "I cook basically what I feel like cooking that day," says Laura. Trust me, you'll like whatever she's having. The cafe's fluffy Tanglewood Pie is famous all over Kentucky for its banana flavor, and the Hot Turkey Salad (there's not a green leaf to be found in it) ranks as one of my favorites. Both will fortify you for a hike in the lush mountains nearby.

Courthouse Cafe Hot Fudge Brownie Sundaes

The brownie is gooey, as it should be, with a nice crust. The homemade syrup is most pourable when it's hot. The ice cream puts it over the top.

Brownies

1	cup butter, melted
⅓	cup vegetable oil
4	large eggs
2	cups sugar
1⅓	cups all-purpose flour
⅔	cup unsweetened cocoa
1¼	tsp. baking powder
½	tsp. salt

Hot Fudge Syrup

½	cup sugar
½	cup light corn syrup
¼	cup unsweetened cocoa
¼	cup heavy cream
2	Tbsp. butter

Other ingredient

1	pint vanilla ice cream

1. Prepare Brownies: Preheat oven to 350°. Whisk together butter and oil in a large bowl. Add eggs, whisking until blended. Stir together sugar and next 4 ingredients in a medium bowl. Stir flour mixture into egg mixture.

2. Pour batter into a lightly greased 13- x 9-inch pan. Bake at 350° for 25 to 28 minutes or until a wooden pick inserted in center comes out with a few moist crumbs. Cool completely on a wire rack (about 1½ hours). Cut brownies into squares.

3. Prepare Hot Fudge Syrup: Stir together all ingredients in a small saucepan; bring to a boil. Reduce heat, and simmer 5 minutes or until thickened.

4. Top each brownie with ice cream and warm Hot Fudge Syrup. **Makes 12 servings.**

Courthouse Cafe Tanglewood Pie

Fluffy and velvety, this banana baby is awesome.
It also comes together in a snap.

1	(9-inch) frozen unbaked piecrust shell
1	cup heavy cream
12	oz. cream cheese, softened
1¼	cups sugar, divided
2	ripe bananas, sliced
1	cup fresh blueberries
1	Tbsp. fresh lime juice
1	Tbsp. butter

1. Bake piecrust shell according to package directions; let cool completely (about 45 minutes).
2. Beat cream at high speed with an electric mixer in a medium bowl until soft peaks form. Beat cream cheese and ¾ cup sugar at medium-high speed with an electric mixer in a large bowl 3 minutes or until smooth. Fold whipped cream into cream cheese mixture. Spread one-third of mixture into piecrust shell; top with sliced bananas. Top with remaining cream cheese mixture. Cover and chill at least 2 hours or until firm.
3. Meanwhile, stir together remaining ½ cup sugar, blueberries, lime juice, and butter in a medium saucepan. Bring to a boil; reduce heat, and simmer 4 to 5 minutes or until blueberries soften and mixture thickens slightly. Serve warm or at room temperature, spooned over pie slices. **Makes 8 servings.**

The Courthouse Cafe

I'm about to rock your world. That's right, because you've bought this book, I'm going to let you in on the next big thing in food. You know, every chef is always pondering what's going to be gracing menus across the country next season—like the rutabaga renaissance of 2003 or the lump crab craze of 2010. Ready to wrap your brain around this? It's cream cheese. You think I'm kidding, but this is going to be big. Cream cheese is everywhere, and, folks, I think it began right here in Whitesburg. No, seriously. Way up here in the hills of Kentucky. Sure, you're pondering, what's so big about cream cheese? Try the Tanglewood Pie and repent, ye doubter. It's going to sweep the nation. You watch.

The Homestead

Winchester, Kentucky

Aside from knowing just about everyone in Kentucky, Megan Smith makes some incredible food. Though she sold The Homestead awhile back—and the lovely pasture-surrounded restaurant has since closed—you can still enjoy her fantastic granola and carrot cake with the recipes here and visit her blog (homemaking101.com) for Megan's tips on cooking, decorating, and more. Fun side note: Megan's preteen son Canaan crafts gourmet marshmallows that make the regular puffed stuff taste like dirt. You can order them at (themarshmallowscompany.com).

1923
⟷
1927
←

BROWNIES
SANDWICHE
HOMEMAD

The Homestead's Famous Granola

Not so chunky that it cracks your dental work, this granola has a great bite and is perfect with Greek yogurt and berries.

4   cups uncooked regular oats
1   cup unsweetened shredded coconut
½   cup vegetable oil
1   Tbsp. ground cinnamon
2   tsp. salt
1   (14-oz.) can sweetened condensed milk

1. Preheat oven to 300°. Toss together all ingredients in a large bowl. Spread onto a parchment paper-lined large baking sheet in a single layer.
2. Bake at 300° for 10 minutes or until golden brown on top. Remove from oven; stir granola. Return to oven, and bake 30 more minutes or until the granola is golden throughout.
3. Cool completely on pan, stirring occasionally. Store at room temperature in an airtight container up to 1 month. **Makes 7¾ cups.**

OVERHEARD: "He could charm a dog off a meat truck." When Sylvia Lovely, cohost of Lexington's Sunny Side Up radio show, described me this way to her listeners, I turned beet red and burst out laughing at the same time. The classic Kentucky expression is one you won't hear anywhere else.

The Homestead's Signature Carrot Cake

Oh, carrot cake. For those of us who love shredded coconut and carrots, this tall and moist version stacks up among the best.

Cake

2	Tbsp. butter

Parchment paper

2⅓	cups all-purpose flour
1½	Tbsp. ground cinnamon
1	Tbsp. ground ginger
2½	tsp. baking powder
1	tsp. salt
½	tsp. baking soda
2	cups sugar
1	cup vegetable oil
4	large eggs
1½	tsp. vanilla extract
2	cups freshly shredded carrots
1	cup unsweetened shredded coconut
¾	cup drained crushed pineapple

Frosting

2	(8-oz.) packages cream cheese, softened
1½	cups butter, softened
3	cups powdered sugar
¼	cup cream of coconut
2	tsp. vanilla extract

1. Prepare Cake: Preheat oven to 350°. Butter 3 (9-inch) pans. Line bottoms of pans with parchment paper.

2. Whisk together flour and next 5 ingredients in a medium bowl. Combine sugar and oil in a bowl of a heavy-duty electric stand mixer; beat at medium speed 1 minute or until well blended. Add eggs, 1 at a time, beating well after each addition. Beat in vanilla. Add flour mixture; beat until blended. Add carrots, coconut, and pineapple; beat until blended.

3. Pour batter into prepared pans. Bake at 350° for 21 to 23 minutes or until a wooden pick inserted in center comes out clean. Cool in pans on wire racks 10 minutes. Gently run a knife around edge of cake layers to loosen, and invert onto wire racks. Cool completely (about 1 hour).

4. Prepare Frosting: Beat cream cheese and butter at medium speed with an electric mixer in a large bowl until smooth. Add powdered sugar, beating until smooth. Add cream of coconut and vanilla; beat just until blended.

5. Place 1 cake layer, flat side up, on a cake stand or serving plate. Spread with ¾ cup frosting; top with second cake layer, flat side up. Spread with ¾ cup frosting. Top with remaining cake layer, rounded side up. Spread top and sides of cake with a thin layer of frosting. Chill cake and remaining frosting 30 minutes.

6. Spread top and sides of cake with remaining frosting. Cover and chill 1 to 12 hours before serving. **Makes 10 to 12 servings.**

Stinky & Coco's Diner

1 North Main Street
Winchester, Kentucky
(859) 744-8100

Farmers in these parts know the laid-back ease of this downtown diner. They come in the predawn darkness to talk crops and politics over hot coffee and hearty fare such as feta eggs and the "Stinky Melt." I've had a lot of feta omelets, but never feta browned in a perfect scramble. The resulting dish has a meaty quality (despite there being no meat in it) and will certainly stick to your ribs while you plant tobacco or tour the charming downtown. Make sure to down an Ale 8 while you're here; a great Winchester tradition, it tastes a bit like a hybrid of ginger ale and lemon-lime soda. (PS: Stinky and Coco are the owner's cats.)

Stinky & Coco's Feta Eggs

Lightly browned and hearty, this scramble is unusual and delicious. Serve with thick slices of buttered sourdough toast.

¼	cup unsalted butter
I	cup diced white onion
I	cup diced green bell pepper
I	cup chopped fresh mushrooms
8	large eggs, lightly beaten
I	tsp. kosher salt
I	tsp. freshly ground pepper
I	lb. crumbled feta cheese
I	cup chopped plum tomatoes

1. Melt butter in a large skillet over medium heat. Add onion, bell pepper, and mushrooms; sauté 2 minutes.

2. Whisk together eggs, salt, and pepper; add to skillet, and sprinkle with feta cheese. Cook, stirring occasionally, until the moisture from the feta is gone and the cheese begins to brown, about 5 minutes. Add tomatoes; cook, stirring often, 2 more minutes or until thoroughly heated. Serve immediately. **Makes 4 servings.**

The Stinky Melt

A cross between a grilled cheese and a burger, this sandwich is a local fave—cheesy, greasy, and perfect!

2   lb. ground chuck
2   Tbsp. vegetable oil
1½   cups chopped onions
12   hearty white bread slices
6   Tbsp. butter, softened
Hot Mayo (below)
18   (1-oz.) processed American cheese slices
Dill pickle slices

1. Shape ground beef into 6 (5-inch) oval patties. Cook 3 patties in 1 Tbsp. hot oil in a large skillet over medium-high heat 4 minutes on each side or until no longer pink in center. Remove patties from skillet, and repeat procedure with remaining patties and oil. Keep warm.
2. Sauté onions in hot drippings over medium-high heat 2 to 3 minutes or until tender.
3. Liberally coat 1 side of each bread slice with butter; turn bread slices over, and liberally coat each bread slice with Hot Mayo. Layer patty, 3 cheese slices, and pickles between bread slices, with the buttered sides facing out. (Pickles should cover the entire sandwich.)
4. In a clean skillet over medium-high heat, grill the sandwiches, in batches, until bread is golden brown and cheese is melted. Serve immediately.
Makes 6 servings.

Hot Mayo

1   cup mayonnaise
¼   cup Asian Sriracha hot chili sauce
1½ Tbsp. fresh lemon juice

1. Stir together all ingredients in a small bowl.
Makes 1 cup.

Windy Corner Market

4595 Bryan Station Road
Lexington, Kentucky
(859) 294-9338

Horses bray just across the street. Winding roads lead visitors through rambling pastures. Windy Corner's graceful design recalls that of an old-time general store, complete with canned goods and a painted mural. Chef and owner Ouita Michel has a reputation for creating first-class restaurants, and Windy Corner is no exception. The market-eatery uses locally grown produce and meats, and celebrates Kentucky with jams, jellies, beer, candies, and a slew of other bluegrass foodstuffs. Give yourself time to linger over a cup of coffee or a platter of artichoke fritters. Windy Corner is just made for relaxing.

Windy Corner Artichoke Fritters

2	(14-oz.) cans quartered artichoke hearts, drained
¼	cup grated Parmesan cheese
¼	cup crumbled feta cheese
¼	cup Dijon mustard
2	Tbsp. minced fresh parsley
2	Tbsp. minced green onion
1	tsp. cider vinegar
¾	tsp. salt
¾	tsp. freshly ground pepper
3	large eggs
¾	cup all-purpose flour

Vegetable oil
Rémoulade (below)

1. Pulse artichoke hearts in a food processor 4 or 5 times or until finely chopped. Transfer to a large bowl. Stir in Parmesan cheese and next 8 ingredients. Add flour, stirring to thicken to a chunky paste.
2. Pour oil to depth of 2 inches in a Dutch oven; heat to 350°. Drop batter by medium (2-Tbsp.) scoops into hot oil, and fry, in batches, 5 to 6 minutes or until golden brown. Drain. Serve hot with Rémoulade. **Makes 2 dozen.**

Rémoulade

1⅓	cups mayonnaise
¼	cup loosely packed fresh parsley leaves, chopped
2	Tbsp. fresh lemon juice
1½	tsp. dried tarragon
1½	tsp. paprika
1	tsp. ground red pepper
2	tsp. drained capers
1	tsp. Creole mustard
1	garlic clove, pressed

1. Stir together all ingredients. **Makes 1½ cups.**

Jared's Beer Cheese Dip

This typical Kentucky delight may startle at first.
It's spicy and thick enough to serve in a lettuce cup
without it running all over on you.

1½	lb. pasteurized prepared cheese product, cut in cubes
2	Tbsp. bourbon
½	cup bourbon ale (beer aged in bourbon barrels)
1½	Tbsp. hot sauce
1½	Tbsp. Worcestershire sauce
1	tsp. onion powder
1	tsp. paprika
1	tsp. garlic powder
1	tsp. ground white pepper
½	tsp. ground red pepper

Crudités and sliced bread

1. Place cheese product and next 2 ingredients in a saucepan over low heat. Cook, stirring occasionally, until cheese is melted and smooth. Stir in hot sauce and next 6 ingredients. Heat through. Serve with crudités and sliced bread. **Makes 5 cups.**

Note: We tested with Velveeta for the cheese product and Harviestoun Ola Dubh for the bourbon ale.

SOUNDTRACK:

• "Prettiest Tree on the Mountain" by Ben Sollee

• "Blue Moon of Kentucky" by Patsy Cline

• "Endless Highway" by Alison Krauss

• "Whiskey in My Whiskey" by Dawes

• "Drunk" by Jimmy Liggins

Hillbilly Hot Dogs

6951 Ohio River Road
Lesage, West Virginia
(304) 762-2458

When you come across the biggest collection of junk this side of the Appalachian Mountains, you've found Hillbilly Hot Dogs. The shack (and I do mean a shack), along with two buses that are now part of the dining room, is held together with rust, used license plates, and redneck proverbs like "It's hotter than a pup's butt in a pepper patch." Owners Sharie and Sonny Knight make sure diners have fun with songs, jokes, and a wild menu of hot dogs loaded with everything from eggs to nachos. The real showstopper is their "Home-Wrecker"—a 15-inch behemoth laden with cheese, peppers, mustard, and just about every other heartburn-inducing substance imaginable. It's awesome. So are the colorfully named Feliz Navidogs.

Feliz Navidogs

These spicy and delicious dogs are named for their Christmasy colors.

6   beef hot dogs
6   hot dog buns, toasted
1½   cups Hillbilly Chili (below)
¾   cup sour cream
2   cups (8 oz.) shredded white Cheddar cheese
3   Tbsp. finely diced red bell pepper
3   Tbsp. finely diced green bell pepper

1. Grill hot dogs according to package directions. Place hot dogs in buns, and top each with ¼ cup chili, 2 Tbsp. sour cream, ⅛ cup cheese, and 1½ Tbsp. each red and green bell pepper. **Makes 6 servings.**

Hillbilly Chili

This fiery concoction is great all by itself, and terrific atop the Feliz Navidogs.

1   green bell pepper
1   yellow bell pepper
1   orange bell pepper
1   red bell pepper
2   lb. ground chuck
½   tsp. vegetable oil
3¾   cups diced tomato
1½   cups diced onion
½   cup diced celery
1½   Tbsp. salt
2   Tbsp. chili powder
1   Tbsp. dried crushed red pepper
2½   Tbsp. liquid from canned jalapeño peppers or liquid from hot peppers in vinegar
1   (12-oz.) can tomato paste
2   (16-oz.) cans dark kidney beans, drained
Shredded Cheddar cheese

1. Dice bell peppers; reserve 3 Tbsp. of each color pepper for topping.

2. Brown ground chuck in hot oil in a 6-qt. Dutch oven over medium-high heat, stirring often, 7 minutes or until meat crumbles and is no longer pink; drain. Add remaining diced bell pepper, tomato, and next 6 ingredients; sauté 5 minutes or until vegetables are crisp-tender. Add tomato paste and 2½ cups water; bring to a boil. Cover, reduce heat, and simmer 30 minutes. Add beans; simmer, uncovered, 1 hour, stirring occasionally. Top each serving with Cheddar cheese and reserved diced bell pepper. **Makes 12 cups.**

Pies & Pints

219 West Maple Avenue
Fayetteville, West Virginia
(304) 574-2200

After a hard day of rock-climbing or
rafting among the stunning vistas of the
Mountain State, power up with carbs
(namely beer and pizza) at this Fayetteville
find. I'm not talking plain old pepperoni
and PBR. No, Pies & Pints boasts a vast
selection of locally brewed beers, as well
as pizzas made with the freshest mozzarella, pesto, garlic, and sausage. Everything
is crafted on-site daily. The specialty pies
should not be missed. My favorite is the
sweet and savory grape pie, made with red
grapes, Gorgonzola, and fresh rosemary.
The creamy chicken Gouda pie is also
popular with the locals. If you save room,
order the chocolate peanut butter brownie
terrine—a dense, crunchy, gooey delight.

Pies & Pints Grape Pie

*Grapes on pizza? With Gorgonzola? And how.
This unusual combination of flavors works well,
and it makes two 8-inch pizzas.*

1   ball Handcrafted Pizza Dough (page 102)
4   tsp. olive oil
½   cup (4 oz.) shredded mozzarella cheese
½   cup (4 oz.) shredded provolone cheese
1   cup halved seedless red grapes
¼   cup crumbled Gorgonzola cheese
1   tsp. chopped fresh rosemary

1. Place a pizza stone or a large baking sheet in
oven. Preheat oven to 500° for 30 to 45 minutes
so that it gets good and hot before you press out
the dough.
2. Cut dough into 2 portions. Stretch 1 portion
of dough into an 8-inch circle on a lightly
floured surface, pressing out dough with the heel
of your hand. With your fingers, form a slightly
thicker raised rim around edge of circles. Repeat
procedure with remaining portion of dough.
3. Transfer each dough circle to a floured pizza
pan or unrimmed baking sheet. Brush dough
circles with oil. Toss together mozzarella and
provolone cheese; sprinkle over dough circles.
Top each with grape halves, Gorgonzola cheese,
and rosemary. Slide pizzas from baking sheet
onto hot pizza stone or baking sheet in oven.
Bake at 500° for 10 to 12 minutes until cheese is
bubbly and edges of crust are golden. **Makes
4 to 6 servings.**

Note: Pizzas may be assembled and baked indi-
vidually if your pizza stone or baking sheet isn't
large enough to accommodate both at once.

OVERHEARD: "He could shoot the whiskers off a gnat."

One's shooting skills are pretty important, particularly in a state as interested in the outdoors as West Virginia. Thus, this expression is usually a compliment. "He couldn't hit the broad side of a barn" means the opposite.

Pies & Pints Handcrafted Pizza Dough

This dough cooks up chewy in the middle and crispy on the outside. Each ball can be stretched to make 1 (12-inch) pizza or 2 (8-inch) pizzas. It can be made and chilled well ahead of when you need it.

1	(¼-oz.) envelope active dry yeast
1½	cups warm water (100° to 110°)
2	Tbsp. extra virgin olive oil
1	Tbsp. honey
4	cups all-purpose flour, plus more for kneading
1	tsp. salt

1. Combine yeast, warm water, oil, and honey in a large bowl; let stand 5 minutes. Gradually stir in flour and salt to make a soft dough. As soon as you can scrape the dough out in one piece, scrape it onto a lightly floured work surface; knead 5 minutes, adding flour as necessary until the dough is smooth and elastic. (Dough will be soft.)

2. Place in a well-greased bowl, turning to grease top. Cover dough with plastic wrap, and let rise in a warm place (85°), free from drafts, 45 minutes or until doubled in bulk.

3. Punch dough down, and shape into a large ball; cut dough into 2 equal pieces. Roll each piece of dough into a ball by gently pulling the dough and tucking each pull under the bottom, working your way around each portion 4 or 5 times. Then, on a smooth, floured surface, roll the ball around under your palm until the ball feels smooth, about 1 minute.

4. Place dough balls on a lightly greased baking sheet, and cover with plastic wrap or a damp towel. Let rest at least 30 minutes. If not using immediately, place each ball in a separate large zip-top plastic freezer bag, and store in refrigerator up to 2 days, or freeze up to 1 month. Thaw frozen dough at room temperature for 2 hours. **Makes 2 dough balls.**

West Virginia

Pies & Pints

There are some poor, lost souls out there who get their pizza from a frozen cardboard circle or, worse, from a smelly carpeted hut near the interstate. Pray for them. Because that's just pitiful, sad, cry-all-your-mascara-down-your-face pizza. Save your Kleenex, and try my favorite pizza in West Virginia. The dough at Pies & Pints is simply fantastic. Co-owner Kimberly Shingledecker (which goes in the registry of cool last names right after Beerswiller and Knifethrower) tried to teach me how to make it. My attempt was nowhere near as good as hers. Ah, but it was still considerably happier than those other alternatives.

SOUNDTRACK:

"Ain't No Sunshine When She's Gone" by Slab Fork native Bill Withers

"Barton Hollow" by the Civil Wars

"The Old Man of the Mountain" by Big Bad Voodoo Daddy

"You Ain't Going Nowhere" by The Byrds

"Sixteen Tons" (oldie but goodie) by Tennessee Ernie Ford

West Virginia

BUSINESS NORTH
LA 1   LA 3191

CLARKSDALE
OXBOW
MISSISSIPPI

KARTCHNER'S
GROCERY & SPECIALTY
MEATS #2

24562 Hwy. 190
Krotz Springs, LA 70750
337-566-0529
Website: kartchnersspecialties.com

PRY OFF CAP
Abita!
BREWED WITH
SPRING WATER

Lasyone's Meat
Pies Restaurant

Kartchner's Grocery
and Specialty Meats

Mandina's
Restaurant

Rocky & Carlo's
Restaurant & Bar

TO the GULF

Alabama • Mississippi • Louisiana

Niki's West ↓

← Oxbow

↖ The Pantry

Lusco's ↓

↙ Grumpy's

← Pie Lab

Sweet P's
Eats and Treats ↓

Queen G's ↓

Blow Fly Inn ↘

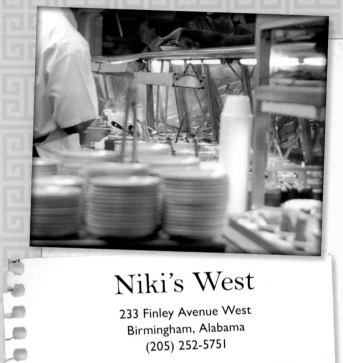

Niki's Greek Chicken

This is a Niki's West classic and the restaurant's most popular dish. The lemon makes it.

1	(4- to 4½-lb.) whole chicken, quartered
3	Tbsp. olive oil
1	Tbsp. minced garlic
3	lemons, cut in half
1	tsp. coarse sea salt
¾	tsp. freshly ground pepper
¼	cup dried oregano

1. Place chicken pieces in a single layer in a 13- x 9-inch baking dish; rub chicken with olive oil and garlic. Squeeze lemons over chicken; sprinkle with salt, pepper, and oregano, liberally coating your bird. Cover and chill at least 2 hours and up to 12 hours.

2. Preheat oven to 350°. Bake chicken, uncovered, for 1 hour and 15 minutes or until a thermometer inserted in thickest part of each quarter registers 165°. Let stand 10 minutes before serving. **Makes 4 servings.**

Niki's West

233 Finley Avenue West
Birmingham, Alabama
(205) 252-5751

There are meat-and-three eateries, and then there's Niki's West. This place has everything that will fly, run, swim, or crawl spread out dead on a table plus about 75 vegetables (if you count mac 'n' cheese and congealed salad as vegetables—as any self-respecting Southerner does). Niki's attracts more than 2,000 diners for lunch and whisks them through the line with startling efficiency. Don't be chitchatting when Tony says "Serve you?" Ordering is serious business. The Greek chicken and fried green tomatoes remain perpetual favorites, but it's the warm banana pudding that will make you weep for joy. Carrie Hudson, whose recipe is revealed for the first time here, has been making it daily since 1957. It's my favorite dessert in the South. Oh, and for best signage, Niki's West wins, hands down, for this gem: "To be served: no bare feet, no tank tops, no rollers on head."

Miss Hudson's Banana Pudding

It's considered a veg at Niki's West, God bless 'em.

1¾ cups sugar

¾ cup all-purpose flour

2¾ cups milk

4 egg yolks

2 Tbsp. vanilla extract

1 (11-oz.) box Nilla Wafers

3 ripe bananas, cut into ¼-inch-thick slices (3 cups)

4 egg whites

¼ cup sugar

⅛ tsp. vanilla extract

1. Preheat oven to 400°. Whisk together sugar and flour in a medium-size heavy saucepan. Gradually whisk in milk until blended. Cook over medium heat, whisking constantly, 5 minutes or until thickened.

2. Whisk egg yolks until thick and pale. Gradually whisk about one-fourth of hot milk mixture into yolks; add yolk mixture to remaining hot milk mixture, whisking constantly. Pour into a clean saucepan. Cook over low heat, whisking constantly, 5 minutes or until thickened. Remove from heat; stir in 2 Tbsp. vanilla. Toss together vanilla wafers and banana slices in an 11- x 7-inch baking dish. Top with warm pudding.

3. Beat egg whites at high speed with an electric mixer until foamy. Gradually add ¼ cup sugar, 1 Tbsp. at a time, beating until stiff peaks form and sugar dissolves (about 2 to 4 minutes). Beat in ⅛ tsp. vanilla with the last tablespoon of sugar. Spread meringue over warm pudding, sealing to edges of dish. Bake at 400° for 8 minutes or until golden brown. Let stand 30 minutes. Serve warm.

Makes 8 to 10 servings.

Niki's West

When I moved home to Birmingham after years of exile in New York City, I gained 15 pounds in about three months. I blame Niki's West. The employees who work the line here know I'm going to order fried green tomatoes, collard greens, English peas, banana pudding, and a yeast roll as big as my noggin every time I walk in the door. And I always eat it all because it's fantabulous. Niki's is more than just a huge cafeteria though. Its tables are where the South comes together. Black, white, rich, poor, investment banker, garbage collector, senior, student, minister, mayor—to the waitresses here, they're all called "sugar." And Niki's West is where you'll find them all tucking into their favorite dishes.

Alabama

The Pantry

17 Dexter Avenue
Birmingham, Alabama
(205) 803-3585

What started as a small take-out shop for the most delicious goat cheese, honey, and jams you've ever stuck in your mouth has blossomed into this hidden Alabama gem. Healthy Southern food? You bet. This pantry brims with fresh marinated tomato sandwiches, heirloom tomato salads, freshly squeezed juices and smoothies, and flavorful desserts. Owners Deborah and Alexandra Stone make it all with locally grown, organic produce, much of it harvested from their own achingly beautiful farm in Harpersville, Alabama. In fact, the Stones make all the goat cheese, honey, and jams. (You can order them at stonehollowfarmstead.com.) I use The Pantry's inventive smoothies to detox from my barbecue, bacon, and fried-everything binges. And all right, fine, when my willpower breaks, I indulge in their goat cheese mini cheesecake.

SOUNDTRACK:

"Holding Steady" by Huntsville singer Shelly Colvin

"Hang Loose" by Alabama Shakes

"It's Hard to Be Humble (when you're from Alabama)" by Phosphorescent

"Sweet Home Alabama" by Lynyrd Skynyrd

"Stars Fell on Alabama" by Randy Newman

"Angel from Montgomery" by Old Crow Medicine Show or by Bonnie Raitt and John Prine

"Birmingham" by Amanda Marshall

The Pantry's Superfruit Smoothie

This sweet and creamy smoothie may fool you into thinking there's ice cream in it. Look for the juices in better grocery and natural food stores. Royal jelly, a honeybee secretion often sold as a dietary supplement, can be found at health-food stores.

2	Tbsp. goji, mangosteen, or noni juice
2	Tbsp. honey
¼	cup blueberries
½	banana
¼	cup plain or vanilla yogurt
3	drops stevia
¼	tsp. royal jelly (optional)
¼	cup coconut water, or more as needed
½	cup ice, or more as needed

1. Place all ingredients in blender, and blend until smooth, adding more coconut water to thin or ice to thicken as needed. **Makes 1 serving.**

The Pantry's Goat Cheese Mini Cheesecakes

Dense and sweet, these are as flavorful as the goat cheese you begin with. If you don't need all four of these sharable cheesecakes at once, wrap the extras in plastic, and then freeze them for up to 1 month.

Crust

Parchment paper

1½ tsp. grapeseed oil

1 cup graham cracker crumbs

½ cup organic sugar

¼ cup European-style butter, softened

Cheesecake

1¼ lb. goat cheese, softened at room temperature

⅔ cup organic sugar

1 Tbsp. lemon zest

6 large eggs, at room temperature

Other Ingredients

Blackberry or other fruit syrup

Garnish: fresh blackberries

1. Prepare Crust: Preheat oven to 325°. Line bottoms of 4 (4½-inch) springform pans with parchment paper; brush paper and sides of pans lightly with grapeseed oil.

2. Stir together graham cracker crumbs and next 2 ingredients; press mixture on bottoms of springform pans. Bake at 325° for 7 minutes. Cool on wire racks. Reduce oven temperature to 300°.

3. Prepare Cheesecake: Beat goat cheese, sugar, and lemon zest at medium speed with a heavy-duty electric stand mixer, using paddle attachment, 2 minutes or until completely smooth. Add eggs, 1 at a time, beating until blended after each addition. Divide batter evenly among prepared crusts.

4. Add hot tap water to a baking pan to depth of 1 inch; place pan on bottom rack of oven. (This will keep the cheesecakes moist and prevent burning around the edges.) Bake cheesecakes at 300° for 30 minutes or until cheesecakes jiggle slightly in the middle when you bump the pans. Remove cheesecakes from oven; gently run a sharp knife around edge of cheesecakes to loosen. Cool completely on a wire rack (about 30 minutes). Cover and chill 8 to 24 hours.

5. Remove sides of pans; run knife under cheesecakes, and remove pan bottoms and parchment. Place cheesecakes on plates; drizzle with fruit syrup. **Makes 8 servings.**

OVERHEARD: "That dog won't hunt."

Alabamians are a practical people, and when something simply won't work or isn't worth the effort, you may hear them make this exclamation. I usually say it when someone offers me unsweetened tea.

Pie Lab

1317 Main Street
Greensboro, Alabama
(334) 624-3899

My four Southern food groups are bourbon, salt, bacon, and pie. And Lord help me, pie is a trap that will catch me every time. I lurve pie. And when there came upon the land a restaurant devoted entirely to pie, lo, this food critic rejoiced. Readers of my first book may remember that Pie Lab, in tiny Greensboro, gave me the recipes for their delicious apple pie, peach pie, and strawberry lemonade. Well, I just couldn't stop there—so I asked Pie Lab for second helpings. Though I'm still trying to get the mad pie scientists to come up with a savory bourbon-and-bacon pie, in the meantime they've forked over the recipe for their famous Butterscotch Pecan Pie. What could be more Southern?

Pie Lab's Butterscotch Pecan Pie

The butterscotch flavor is subtle, adding an interesting twist without overwhelming this Southern classic. And the experts at Pie Lab have ensured that the filling fits the piecrust perfectly.

½ (14.1-oz.) package refrigerated piecrusts (or 1 homemade 9-inch piecrust, rolled to ⅛-inch thickness)
¾ cup firmly packed brown sugar
¾ cup dark corn syrup
2 Tbsp. all-purpose flour
1 tsp. vanilla extract
3 large eggs, lightly beaten
3 Tbsp. butter, melted
1½ cups pecan halves
½ cup butterscotch morsels

1. Preheat oven to 350°. Fit piecrust into a 9-inch pie plate according to package directions; fold edges under, and crimp.
2. Whisk together brown sugar and next 4 ingredients in a large bowl until smooth. Whisk in melted butter. Stir in pecans and butterscotch morsels. Pour mixture into piecrust.
3. Bake at 350° for 50 minutes or until set and slightly puffed. Cool completely on a wire rack (about 4 hours). **Makes 8 servings.**

Sweet P's
Eats and Treats

11775 Troy Highway
Pike Road, Alabama
(334) 288-4900

As you motor past farms and fields along the Troy Highway, keep an eye out for this quaint cabin tucked in a pine knoll just off the road. Don't let its distinctly rural location fool you: Sweet P's dishes out cupcakes and other delectables every bit as tasty and inventive as Magnolia's in New York City. For an entire country-boy breakfast in one bite, chomp down on the bacon-and-pancake cupcake. Or for the richest, most gooey brownie, opt for the Cow Patty. If it's not too hot outside, claim a rocking chair on the front porch.

Sweet P's Cinnamon Pancake Cupcakes with Maple-Bacon Buttercream Frosting

Are these breakfast or dessert? You be the judge. Either way, the frosting is seriously scrumptious.

Cupcakes

4	cups all-purpose soft-wheat flour
¼	cup sugar
4	tsp. baking powder
2	tsp. salt
2	tsp. ground cinnamon
1½	cups milk
4	large eggs
½	cup unsalted butter, melted
	Paper baking cups
	Vegetable cooking spray

Frosting

2	cups unsalted butter, softened
5	cups powdered sugar
6	Tbsp. pure maple syrup
2	tsp. vanilla extract
¼	cup cooked and crumbled bacon slices
8	cooked bacon slices, each broken into thirds

1. **Prepare Cupcakes:** Preheat oven to 400°. Whisk together flour and next 4 ingredients in a large bowl. Make a well in center of mixture. Whisk together milk and eggs in a medium bowl; stir in melted butter. Add milk mixture to flour mixture, stirring just until dry ingredients are moistened.

2. Place paper baking cups in 2 (12-cup) muffin pans, and coat with cooking spray; spoon batter into cups, filling two-thirds full.

3. Bake at 400° for 10 to 12 minutes or until puffed and just firm to the touch. Cool in pans on wire racks 5 minutes. Remove from pans to

Queen G's
Charbroiled Oysters

Easy, rich, and delicious, this dish is best cooked in cast-iron skillets (four small or one large), but any broiler-safe pans will do. Select plump oysters; they will shrink a bit.

1   cup finely shredded Parmesan cheese
1   pt. fresh select oysters, drained
¼   tsp. ground red pepper or Cajun seasoning
¼   cup roasted garlic butter with oil
Hard rolls or French baguettes
Garnish: sliced green onions

1. Preheat broiler with oven rack 6 inches from heat.
2. Toss together cheese and oysters in a medium bowl. Divide oysters between 4 (6-inch) cast-iron skillets. Sprinkle evenly with red pepper or Cajun seasoning, and dot with butter.
3. Broil 6 inches from heat 5 minutes just until edges of oysters begin to curl and cheese is browning and bubbling. Serve with hard roll.
Makes 4 servings.

Note: We tested with Land O Lakes Roasted Garlic Butter with Oil.

Queen G's

2518 Old Shell Road
Mobile, Alabama
(251) 471-3361

Queen G's founder, Gaynell Mathers, was Queen of the Polka Dot Mardi Gras in Mobile, where Mardi Gras in the United States originated. Her daughter, Carolyn Mathers, nods to Mama's royal past with polka dots in the decor of her whimsical restaurant, a smallish place in downtown Mobile. You'll probably have to wait if you arrive in the middle of the lunch rush. But not to worry: Carolyn's crew is as polite and Southern as a glass of sweet tea. OK, and they're a tad zany. Feel free to wear your own tiara.

Queen G's Roasted Roots

This solid side dish is a welcome detour from coleslaw in cooler months.

4   medium turnips, peeled, halved crosswise, and cut into ½-inch-thick wedges
1   (16-oz.) package baby carrots
2   Tbsp. olive oil
1   tsp. salt
½   tsp. freshly ground pepper
¼   tsp. dried thyme
¼   tsp. dried oregano
¼   cup unsalted butter, cut into pieces
¼   tsp. minced garlic
2   large shallots, quartered lengthwise

1. Preheat oven to 425°. Toss together turnips and next 6 ingredients in a large, shallow roasting pan; spread vegetables in a single layer. Dot with butter.
2. Bake at 425° for 30 minutes, stirring after 15 minutes. Stir in garlic and shallots. Bake 15 more minutes or until vegetables are caramelized and tender. **Makes 8 servings.**

wire racks, and cool completely (about 20 minutes).

4. Prepare Frosting: Beat butter at medium-high speed with a heavy-duty electric stand mixer, using whisk attachment, 3 minutes or until fluffy and creamy, stopping to scrape down sides. Add powdered sugar, 1 cup at a time, beating at low speed until blended after each addition. When all the powdered sugar is incorporated, whip on medium-high 1 minute or until fluffy. Add maple syrup and vanilla, and whip 1 more minute or until blended. Stir in crumbled bacon.

5. Pipe or spread cupcakes with frosting. Top each with a bacon piece. **Makes 2 dozen.**

Sweet P's Cowboy Cookies

Sweet P's owner, Kadra Parkman, got this recipe from her aunt Carol Starling, who was a trip chef in the Grand Canyon in the '70s. She would bake these cookies before the trips because they're packed full of goodness and would stay fresh for several days.

¾	cup firmly packed light brown sugar
½	cup unsalted butter
1	large egg
2	Tbsp. vanilla extract
¾	cup coarsely chopped dried dates
1	cup all-purpose soft-wheat flour
½	tsp. baking soda
½	tsp. salt
¼	tsp. baking powder
1¾	cups semisweet chocolate morsels
¾	cup coarsely chopped walnuts
½	cup sweetened flaked coconut
½	cup plain granola

1. Preheat oven to 350°. Beat brown sugar and butter at medium speed with an electric mixer 3 minutes or until creamy. Add egg and vanilla, beating well. Stir in dates; let stand 5 minutes to soften dates. Beat at high speed 3 minutes or until very light brown and creamy. Whisk together flour, baking soda, salt, and baking powder in a small bowl; add to butter mixture, beating until blended. Stir in chocolate morsels, and remaining ingredients.

2. Drop large (3-Tbsp.) scoops of dough 2 inches apart onto lightly greased baking sheets. Pat dough down. (One good pat is sufficient. Don't press flat, or the cookie will come out too thin. It tastes best a little thick!)

3. Bake at 350° for 15 minutes or until lightly browned. Cool on baking sheets 15 minutes. (These are gooey in the middle and need time to set.) Transfer to wire racks. **Makes 16 cookies.**

Sweet P's Cow Patties

About the only thing these decadent chocolate concoctions have in common with their namesake is that they're dairy-farm fresh. The filling is incredibly luscious.

Chocolate Cake

Vegetable cooking spray

Parchment paper

2½ cups sugar

2¼ cups all-purpose soft-wheat flour

¾   cup Dutch process cocoa

2   tsp. baking soda

1   tsp. salt

1   cup canola oil

1   cup sour cream

2   Tbsp. white vinegar

1   tsp. vanilla extract

2   large eggs

Swiss Meringue Buttercream Filling

1   cup plus 2 Tbsp. sugar

½   tsp. salt

5   egg whites, at room temperature

2   cups unsalted butter, cut into tablespoons and softened

1¾ tsp. vanilla extract

Chocolate Topping

4   cups sugar

½   cup unsweetened cocoa

1   cup milk

1   cup unsalted butter

2   tsp. vanilla extract

1. Prepare Chocolate Cake: Preheat oven to 350°. Coat an 18- x 13-inch half-sheet pan with cooking spray; line bottom of pan with parchment paper, and coat paper with cooking spray.

2. Sift together sugar, flour, cocoa, baking soda, and salt into bowl of a heavy-duty electric stand mixer. Add oil and sour cream, and beat at low speed, using paddle attachment, until just combined. Gradually beat in 1½ cups water at low speed. Add vinegar and vanilla, beating until blended. Add eggs; beat at medium-low until blended after each addition, stopping to scrape bowl as needed. Pour batter into prepared pan.

3. Bake at 350° for 30 minutes or until a wooden pick inserted in center comes out clean. Cool completely in pan on a wire rack (about 45 minutes).

4. Prepare Swiss Meringue Buttercream Filling: Combine sugar, salt, and egg whites in a large heatproof bowl of a stand mixer. Place bowl over a large saucepan of simmering water. Whisk constantly, by hand, 3 minutes or until a thermometer registers 160° and sugar is dissolved (test by rubbing a little of the mixture between your fingertips; if you don't feel sugar granules, it is ready to move to the stand mixer). Attach the bowl to the mixer; beat at low speed, using whisk attachment, and gradually increase to medium-high speed. Beat until mixture is fluffy and glossy and completely cool (about 4 to 5 minutes). With the mixer at medium speed, add butter, a few tablespoons at a time, beating well after each addition. Once all butter has been added, beat in vanilla.

5. Prepare Chocolate Topping: Whisk together sugar and cocoa in a large saucepan. Gradually whisk in milk until smooth; add butter. Bring to a boil over medium-high heat. Boil 2 minutes, stirring constantly. Fill a large bowl with ice. Place saucepan in ice, and let stand, stirring constantly, until mixture is cool and the consistency of soft caramel (about 3 minutes). Stir in vanilla.

6. Invert cake onto a parchment paper-lined work surface. Gently remove parchment paper from cake bottom, and cut cake into 24 squares (about

3¼- x 3-inches each). Place 1 cake square in a small aluminum pie plate or deep plate; spread with about ⅓ cup Swiss Meringue Buttercream Filling, and top with another cake square (to make a sandwich). Pour about ⅓ cup Chocolate Topping over cake, letting it drip over sides and into bottom of plate. Repeat procedure with remaining Chocolate Cake, Swiss Meringue Buttercream Filling, and Chocolate Topping. Serve immediately. **Makes 12 servings.**

Blow Fly Inn

1201 Washington Avenue
Gulfport, Mississippi
(228) 896-9812

I'm a Navy guy, and when I returned to the good ol' U.S. of A. after being deployed to Afghanistan, I touched down in Gulfport. Aside from a hot shower and a hug from my mama, there was one thing I really, really wanted: a fine cheeseburger. And lordamercy, does the Blow Fly Inn have that. It's not an inn, and you won't find many flies, but you will find a great menu full of fresh seafood and some of the best burgers in the South. Briefly wiped off the map by Hurricane Katrina, the Blow Fly Inn has been completely rebuilt and stands on tall stilts overlooking Bayou Bernard. Don't let the pristine setting fool you: It's still a down-home spot worthy of a lazy Mississippi afternoon.

Blow Fly Inn Pimiento Cheese Burgers

Creamy and spicy, the pimiento cheese adds just the right kick to this burger. Use any leftover cheese in finger sandwiches or as a dip with celery sticks and crackers.

3   lb. ground chuck
1   tsp. salt
1   tsp. freshly ground black pepper
2   cups Roasted Red Pepper Pimiento
     Cheese (below)
6   kaiser rolls
Toppings: mayonnaise, lettuce, tomato slices,
     red onion slices, pickle chips

1. Combine ground chuck, salt, and pepper gently. Shape into 6 (4½-inch) patties. Cook 3 patties in a large skillet over medium-high heat 8 minutes on each side or until no longer pink in center. Top each patty with ⅓ cup pimiento cheese; cover and cook 1 more minute or just until cheese melts. Remove from skillet; keep warm. Repeat procedure with remaining 3 patties and ⅓ cup pimiento cheese per patty. Serve on kaiser rolls with mayonnaise, lettuce, tomato, onion, and pickles. **Makes 6 burgers.**

Roasted Red Pepper Pimiento Cheese

3   large red bell peppers
1   lb. sharp Cheddar cheese, shredded
1   (3-oz.) package cream cheese, softened
½   cup mayonnaise
1   tsp. sugar
1   tsp. ground white pepper
⅛   tsp. ground red pepper
Dash of hot sauce

1. Roast red peppers directly over a gas flame, turning occasionally, 11 minutes or until peppers look blistered. Place peppers in a large zip-top plastic freezer bag; seal bag, and let stand 10 minutes to loosen skins. Peel peppers; remove and discard seeds. Mince peppers.

2. Stir together peppers and next 7 ingredients in a large bowl. Cover and chill at least 1 hour or up to 3 days. **Makes 5⅔ cups.**

Note: If you don't have a gas cooktop with an open flame, broil peppers on an aluminum foil-lined baking sheet 5 inches from heat 5 minutes on each side or until peppers look blistered.

Blow Fly Inn Seafood Pasta with Monica Sauce

This rich dish is like the whole Gulf in a bowl.

Monica Sauce

2	cups heavy cream
½	cup bottled clam juice
1½	tsp. Old Bay seasoning
½	tsp. ground red pepper
½	cup butter
½	cup all-purpose flour

Seafood Pasta

10	asparagus spears
½	lb. unpeeled, large raw shrimp
1	(16-oz.) package penne pasta
2	Tbsp. butter
3	Tbsp. chopped garlic (9 cloves)
1	cup dry white wine
1	(1-lb.) package frozen cooked, peeled crawfish tails, thawed and drained
18	shucked fresh oysters
2	oz. fresh jumbo lump crabmeat (optional)
1	Tbsp. Creole seasoning

Garnish: minced fresh parsley

1. Prepare Monica Sauce: Bring first 4 ingredients and 1 cup water to a boil in a medium saucepan over high heat, whisking often. Reduce heat to medium-low; keep warm.

2. Melt butter in a large skillet over medium heat; gradually whisk in flour, and cook, whisking constantly, until flour is a blond color (about 5 minutes; do not let darken). Gradually whisk roux into cream mixture, and cook, stirring constantly, 2 to 3 minutes or until thickened. Keep warm while you make the pasta.

3. Prepare Seafood Pasta: Snap off and discard tough ends of asparagus. Cook asparagus in boiling salted water to cover 1 minute or just until bright green; drain. Plunge asparagus into ice water to stop the cooking process; drain. Cut into 2-inch pieces. Peel shrimp; devein, if desired.

4. Prepare pasta according to package directions. Meanwhile, melt butter in a 12-inch skillet over medium-high heat. Add garlic, and sauté 1 minute. Add wine; cook 1 minute. Add asparagus, shrimp, crawfish, oysters, and crabmeat, if desired; sprinkle with Creole seasoning. Cook, stirring constantly, 4 minutes or just until shrimp turn pink. Stir in Monica Sauce, and cook, stirring constantly, 2 minutes or until thoroughly heated. Serve over hot pasta. **Makes 6 servings.**

OVERHEARD: "The dinner bell is always in tune."

In the Deep South, "dinner" means lunch. And "supper" means dinner. Got that? Good. Now that we've cleared up what meal we're talking about, when a spread of fried chicken, green beans, potato salad, and pie is waiting for you, there's no sweeter sound than Mama ringing the bell to come inside.

Grumpy's

105 Dr. Martin Luther King Jr. Drive West
Starkville, Mississippi
(662) 323-1132

"Welcome to Grumpy's!" the sign proclaims. "Lousy service, hot beer, bad food." You can't say that this Starkville joint over-promises. Truth is, Grumpy's is an incredibly friendly spot, serving lots of very cold beer and delicious, reasonably priced food in this college town. A lot of the menu is fried. But I'll tell you what: These are some of the lightest and crispiest fried shrimp, fried pickles, and fried green tomatoes I've ever tried. I begged for the beer batter recipe. Fortunately, it's simple and easy to master. You could fry a dishrag in it, and I'd probably eat it (and like it too).

Grumpy's Beer Batter

Light, flaky, and very pale in color, this tempura-like batter works with just about anything. You'll have enough to coat about 4 pounds of food. Try it with dill pickle slices, sliced fresh veggies, or shrimp. When the shrimp and veggies come out of the oil, give them a shake of salt. Pickles are plenty salty without any extra seasoning.

1   cup all-purpose flour, plus more for dredging
1   tsp. Cajun seasoning
1   (12-oz.) can beer (the cheaper, the better)
1   large egg
Vegetable oil for frying
Dill pickle slices, peeled shrimp, or sliced vegetables
      to fry
Ranch dressing for dipping

1. Whisk together first 4 ingredients in a medium bowl.
2. Pour oil to depth of 2 inches in a Dutch oven; heat to 350°. Dip item to be fried in batter; dredge in flour. (Stir batter as needed between dipping.) Fry in hot oil until batter is pale gold. Serve with Ranch dressing. **Makes 2 cups.**

Grumpy's Stuffed Mushrooms

This hot appetizer is gooey and rich, perfect for a game-day snack.

2   (16-oz.) packages fresh mushrooms
¾   lb. hot ground pork sausage
2   Tbsp. diced white onion
2   Tbsp. diced green bell pepper
2   Tbsp. diced red bell pepper
2   Tbsp. diced yellow bell pepper
2   (3-oz.) packages cream cheese, softened
4   tsp. Italian-seasoned breadcrumbs
½   cup (2 oz.) shredded sharp Cheddar cheese
Garnish: sliced green onions
Ranch dressing for dipping (optional)

1. Gently wash mushrooms, and remove stems. Finely chop stems to measure ⅔ cup. Reserve remaining mushroom stems for another use.
2. Brown sausage in a large skillet over medium-high heat, stirring often, 7 minutes or until sausage crumbles and is no longer pink. Drain sausage, reserving 2½ Tbsp. drippings in skillet.

3. Sauté reserved ⅔ cup mushroom stems, onion, and next 3 ingredients in hot drippings over medium-high heat 5 to 7 minutes or until tender. Remove from heat. Stir in sausage, cream cheese, and breadcrumbs.
4. Preheat oven to 350°. Spoon sausage mixture evenly into mushroom caps; place on a lightly greased jelly-roll pan, and sprinkle with Cheddar cheese. Bake at 350° for 15 minutes or until mushrooms are tender and cheese is melted. Serve warm with ranch dressing, if desired.
Makes 3½ dozen.

SOUNDTRACK:

"Always Lookin'" and "Give It Away/Hard Times" by Blue Mother Tupelo
"Mississippi" by JJ Grey & Mofro
"She's Jailbait" by Champion Jack Dupree
"Boom Boom" by John Lee Hooker
"Southern Girl" by Amos Lee
"Mississippi Lady" by Jim Croce

Lusco's

722 Carrollton Avenue
Greenwood, Mississippi
(662) 453-5365

This stretch of the Mississippi River Delta grows eccentric characters like Georgia grows peaches. They're the people who give this otherwise flat farming region its rich music, stories, and food. Chief among its notable eateries sits Lusco's, a legendary spot that has fattened up generations of visitors looking for excellent steaks, fresh pompano, and classic dishes such as owner Karen Pinkston's eggplant Romano. It's an eclectic place: over here, a stuffed squirrel smoking a cigarette; over yonder, a refrigerator (still in use) that dates to President Wilson's administration. Lusco's sells beer and wine, and you can bring your own booze to drink in the private, curtained booths. My favorite bit of lore about the place came from the last thing famed Mississippi writer Willie Morris ever penned. The note simply said, "Gone to Lusco's." We should all be so lucky.

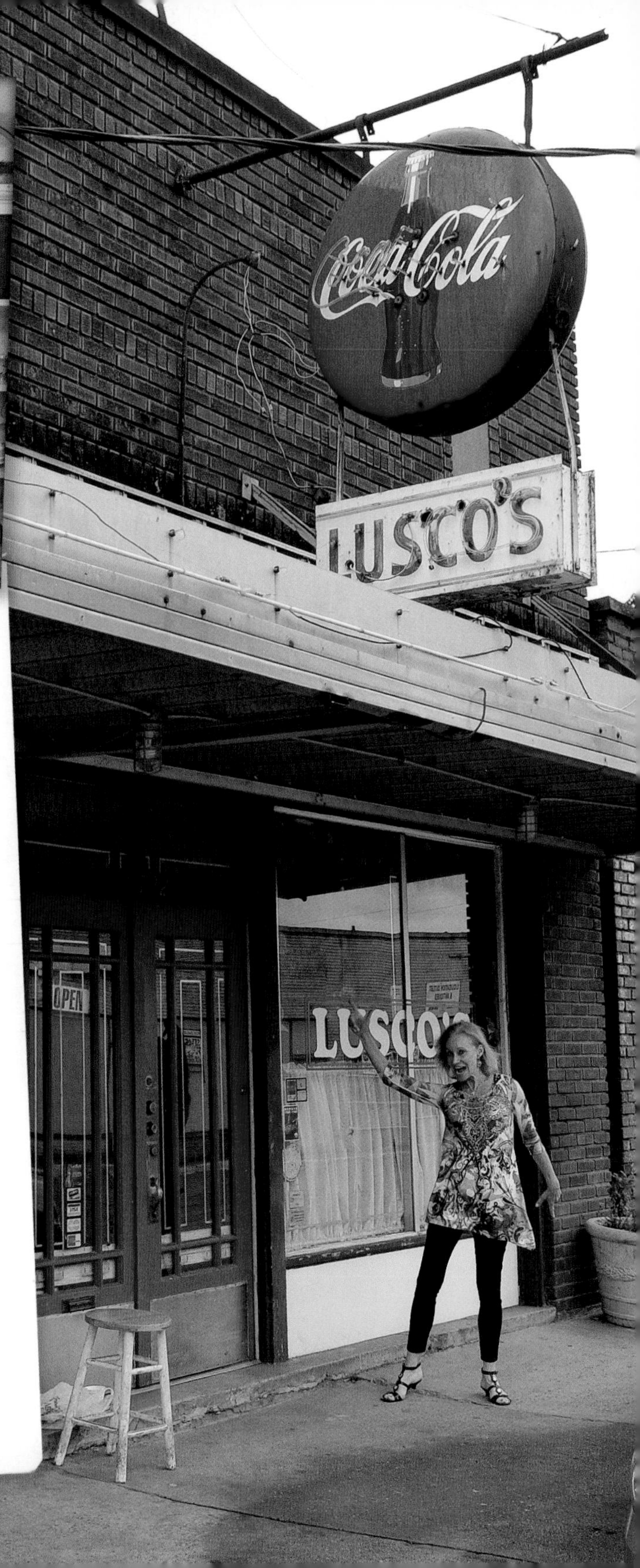

Lusco's Eggplant Romano

This simple dish has a fresh basil flavor and a touch of heat.

1   (14.5-oz.) can whole tomatoes
⅓   cup thinly sliced basil leaves (8 to 10 large leaves)
4   tsp. salt, divided
1½ Tbsp. sugar
2   Tbsp. minced jalapeño pepper
1   Tbsp. extra virgin olive oil
3   medium eggplants (about 3½ lb.), peeled and cut into ¼-inch slices
½   cup vegetable oil
2   cups freshly grated Romano cheese

1. Pulse tomatoes in a food processor 12 times. (Don't overprocess. Tomatoes should still be a bit chunky.) Pour into a small saucepan; stir in basil, 1 tsp. salt, and next 3 ingredients. Cook over low heat 30 minutes or until mixture slightly thickens, stirring occasionally.

2. Meanwhile, sprinkle remaining 3 tsp. salt over both sides of eggplant slices; place slices on layers of paper towels, and let stand 30 minutes. Pat dry with paper towels.

3. Brush both sides of eggplant slices with vegetable oil. Cook eggplant, in batches, in a large nonstick skillet over medium heat 2 minutes on each side or until golden brown and tender.

4. Preheat oven to 350°. Layer half each of eggplant, tomato sauce, and Romano cheese in an 11- x 7-inch baking dish. Repeat layers once. Bake at 350° for 20 minutes or until cheese is melted. **Makes 6 to 8 servings.**

Lusco's Oreo Cheesecake

This is creamy and rich but lighter than it sounds.

1 (15.5-oz.) package cream-filled chocolate sandwich cookies
3 (8-oz.) packages cream cheese, softened
1 cup sugar
2 cups sour cream
2 tsp. vanilla extract
3 large eggs
Garnish: whipped cream

1. Preheat oven to 325°. Wrap aluminum foil around outside of a lightly greased 9-inch springform pan. Process 26 cookies in a food processor 30 seconds or until finely ground. Press cookie crumbs on bottom and 1½ inches up sides of prepared pan.
2. Beat cream cheese and sugar at medium speed with an electric mixer until blended. Add sour cream and vanilla, beating at low speed until well blended. Add eggs, 1 at a time, beating just until yellow disappears after each addition. Pour batter into prepared crust.
3. Break remaining 13 cookies into large pieces. Sprinkle cookies over cheesecake batter, pushing cookies down into batter with a rubber spatula or the back of a spoon. (Do not push cookies too deep. You want the cookies to be thoroughly coated with batter and just under the surface.)
4. Place springform pan in a large shallow pan; pour hot tap water (about 115°) to depth of 1 inch into large pan.
5. Bake at 325° for 1 hour and 15 minutes or until center is almost set. Turn off oven. Let cheesecake stand in oven, with door partially open, 1 hour. Remove cheesecake from oven, and gently run a knife around outer edge of cheesecake to loosen from sides of pan. (Do not remove sides of pan.) Cool on a wire rack 2 hours. Cover and chill 8 to 24 hours. Remove sides of pan. **Makes 10 to 12 servings.**

Oxbow

115 Third Street
Clarksdale, Mississippi
(662) 627-6781

With rusty tin and discarded wooden pallets, homemade light fixtures, and dad's old hi-fi system, Oxbow proves that you needn't spend a million bucks to open a first-class restaurant. Hayden and Erica Hall call their found-object decorating style "our way of recycling." It's incredibly cool. And the cuisine at their restaurant, my favorite gem in Clarksdale, flies first class all the way. Hayden worked for Wolfgang Puck and Susan Spicer, and Oxbow has developed a loyal following for everything from its tuna tacos to its tremendous burgers. My dainty mama, whom I brought along for a visit, devoured every bite of Oxbow's incredible burger. The recipe is a tad involved—but, man, is this baby worth it! The restaurant name is a nod to the Halls' return home to Clarksdale. In river parlance, an oxbow is a dramatic U-shaped bend where a river ends its meandering and returns to its original path. We're all lucky the Halls meandered home.

EAT

Oxbow Burger Stand Burgers

These are smothered in awesome and so good that I almost slapped my mama (because she ate all of mine).

1½ lb. ground chuck
½ tsp. kosher salt
½ tsp. freshly ground pepper
Balsamic Shallot Jam (page 136)
2 oz. smoked Gruyère cheese slices
1 (10.8-oz.) package Hawaiian sweet sandwich buns
Garlicky Mayo Spread (page 136)
1 cup firmly packed romaine lettuce-spring mix blend
16 Quickles (page 137)

1. Heat a cast-iron grill pan over medium-high heat. Shape ground beef into 4 (¾-inch-thick) patties. Use your fingers to make a shallow indentation in the top of each patty. (This will prevent overplumping during cooking.) Sprinkle patties with salt and pepper. Cook patties with the indentations facing up 6 to 7 minutes. Flip patties, and cook 3 to 4 minutes. Top each patty with about 1 Tbsp. Balsamic Shallot Jam and one-fourth of cheese; cook 3 more minutes. Remove patties from grill pan; keep warm.
2. Place buns, cut sides down, on grill pan 30 to 50 seconds or until lightly toasted, pressing them down onto pan for even cooking. Spread Garlicky Mayo on cut sides of buns. Divide lettuce among bottom bun halves. Top with burgers, Quickles, and top bun halves. **Makes 4 burgers.**

Balsamic Shallot Jam

1   cup chopped shallots (about 3)
1   Tbsp. olive oil
1   Tbsp. ketchup
1   Tbsp. balsamic vinegar
¼   tsp. kosher salt
⅛   tsp. freshly ground pepper

1. Sauté shallots in hot oil in a medium skillet over medium-high heat 4 minutes or until translucent. Add ketchup and balsamic vinegar; cook, stirring constantly, 5 minutes or until liquid is thick and shallots are very tender. (You may need to add a little water if it starts to stick.) Remove from heat; cool 10 minutes.
2. Process shallot mixture in a food processer until smooth. Stir in salt and pepper. **Makes ⅓ cup.**

Garlicky Mayo Spread

¼   cup mayonnaise
¼   tsp. Dijon mustard
¼   tsp. yellow mustard
¼   tsp. granulated garlic

1. Stir together all ingredients in a small bowl. **Makes ¼ cup.**

MAKE TACOS ;

Quickles

These quick pickles don't require Mason jars or a canning pot. Just cover and store them in the refrigerator for up to 3 weeks.

1	English cucumber
1	cup white vinegar
1	cup cider vinegar
¼	cup sugar
2	Tbsp. salt
¼	tsp. pickling spice
¼	tsp. chopped fresh dill
1	bay leaf

1. Cut cucumber into ⅛-inch slices using a mandoline or V-slicer, and place in a large glass bowl. Bring 2 cups water, vinegars, and next 5 ingredients to a boil in a medium-size nonreactive saucepan, stirring often, until sugar and salt dissolve.
2. Pour hot vinegar mixture over cucumber slices. Cool to room temperature (about 3 hours). Cover and chill at least 24 hours; store in refrigerator up to 3 weeks. **Makes 2½ cups.**

Oxbow

I'm a sentimental Southerner. It's why I drive sputtery vintage Cadillacs, write love letters with a leaky fountain pen, and still insist on wearing my seersucker suit with a tie in the summertime. Some of the best things take a little extra effort. Likewise, my favorite restaurant in Mississippi has a sentimental streak. The owner's father's artwork lines the walls. A huge, unopened safe that came with the place was saved, even though it's completely useless. That Southern staple, baloney, long discarded by fancy-pants restaurants, makes a gourmet debut here. (I know "gourmet baloney" sounds as oxymoronic as "airline food," "civil war," or "French deodorant"—but it really is good.) The recipes have multiple components but, like much of life, they are worth the effort. And when your guests say, "YOU made this?" just respond coolly, "Yes. Yes, I did. It was no trouble at all." Or something like that.

Kartchner's Grocery and Specialty Meats

24562 Highway 190
Krotz Springs, Louisiana
(337) 566-0529

Boudin is best eaten in the parking lot where you bought it. Kartchner's gravel lot brims with pickups and people buying provisions for family dinners, backyard cookouts, and football games. Like so many shops along Louisiana's highways, Kartchner's sells everything from boudin balls to cracklings and beer. But what sets Kartchner's apart is its vacuum-packed Cajun meals. "In Louisiana, if we can grab it, we'll stuff it," says chef Jordan Leger. "I could wrap limestone with bacon, and it'd be worth selling." He shared recipes for his crawfish étouffée and bacon-wrapped pork tenderloin. If you don't feel like cooking them, place an order at www.kartchnersspecialties.com, and the store will ship them to you.

Kartchner's Crawfish Étouffée

This dish offers color and comfort with authentic Cajun kick. The cream of celery and mushroom soups provide an elegant cheat for the cook, yielding a creamy result without a roux.

½	cup butter
3	cups diced onion
1½	cups diced celery
1½	cups chopped green bell pepper
1	(10-oz.) can diced tomatoes and green chiles
3	Tbsp. dried parsley flakes
1	Tbsp. salt
1	tsp. garlic powder
¾	tsp. ground red pepper
¾	tsp. freshly ground black pepper
1	(10¾-oz.) can cream of celery soup
1	(10¾-oz.) can cream of mushroom soup
4	(1-lb.) packages frozen cooked, peeled crawfish tails, thawed and undrained
¾	cup sliced green onions

Hot cooked white rice
Garnish: sliced green onions

1. Melt butter in a large Dutch oven over medium heat. Add onion and next 8 ingredients; cook, stirring occasionally, 30 minutes or until liquid from vegetables reduces and vegetables begin to brown and stick to the bottom of the pot. Add 2 Tbsp. water, and stir up the browned bits. Stir in soups; bring to a simmer. Add crawfish tails and ¾ cup green onions; simmer, stirring occasionally, 20 minutes or until thoroughly heated. Serve over rice. **Makes 12 servings.**

KARTCHNER'S
GROCERY & SPECIALTY
MEATS #2
24592 Hwy 190
Krotz Springs, LA 70750
337-888-0829
Website: kartchnersspecialties

Kartchner's Grocery

BOUDIN • CRACKLINS
CAJUN
GROCERY •

Kartchner's Bacon-Wrapped Pork Tenderloin

This is the love child of a jalapeño popper and a pork tenderloin: crispy, creamy, smoky, and spicy—with just enough cheese to cut the burn.

1	lb. pork tenderloin
8	slices applewood-smoked bacon
1	(3-oz.) package cream cheese
½	cup chopped, seeded jalapeño pepper

Cajun seasoning

1. Preheat oven to 350°. Butterfly the pork tenderloin, slicing it nearly in half lengthwise and folding it open like a book. Lay it crosswise over the bacon slices. Cut cream cheese into 4 strips. Lay them end-to-end in the center seam of the tenderloin. Top cream cheese with chopped jalapeño. Sprinkle with Cajun seasoning. Fold tenderloin closed, and wrap with bacon to hold filling in. Secure bacon with wooden picks. Sprinkle liberally with Cajun seasoning.

2. Lightly sear tenderloin on all sides in a hot skillet over medium-high heat, cooking 6 minutes or until bacon is about half-done.

3. Transfer tenderloin to a rack on a foil-lined baking sheet. Bake at 350° for 25 minutes or until bacon is crisp and a meat thermometer inserted in center of pork registers 145°. Remove picks. Let rest 5 minutes before slicing. **Makes 4 servings.**

Louisiana

Lasyone's

622 Second Street
Natchitoches, Louisiana
(318) 352-3353

South America has empanadas, Great
Britain has the Cornish pasty, and tiny
Natchitoches boasts the meat pie. Since
1968 Lasyone's meat pies have enthralled
legions of diners at this classic restaurant
in the city's historic downtown. Owners
and sisters Angela and Tina Lasyone hold
their dad's secret meat pie recipe close.
I thought seriously about stealing it but
settled instead for their fried string beans,
red beans and rice, and excellent bread pudding (which uses something every bachelor
has around: old hot dog buns).

Lasyone's Famous Fried String Beans

Marginally better for you than French fries and similar to vegetable tempura, these string beans boast a crispy fried shell.

3¾   cups all-purpose flour
2½   tsp. salt, divided
2½   tsp. granulated garlic, divided
½   tsp. ground red pepper, divided
2   tsp. white vinegar
1   large egg
1   Tbsp. baking powder
Vegetable oil
1   lb. fresh green beans, trimmed
Creole seasoning to taste
Ranch dressing

1. Whisk together flour, 1¼ tsp. salt, 1¼ tsp. garlic, and ¼ tsp. ground red pepper in a medium bowl.
2. Stir together 1½ cups water, remaining 1¼ tsp. salt, 1¼ tsp. garlic, ¼ tsp. ground red pepper, and vinegar in another medium bowl. Whisk together egg and baking powder; whisk into water mixture.
3. Pour oil to depth of 2 inches into a large Dutch oven; heat to 350°.
4. Dip beans, in batches, in egg mixture; dredge in flour mixture. Dip beans again in egg mixture, and dredge once more in flour mixture, shaking off excess. Fry beans, in batches, in hot oil 3 to 4 minutes or until golden brown.
5. Sprinkle beans with Creole seasoning, and serve with Ranch dressing for dipping. **Makes 6 servings.**

Lasyone's Red Beans & Rice

This Louisiana classic is a robust dish that will feed a lot of folks for just a few bucks.

1	lb. dried light red kidney beans
8	oz. smoked sausage, sliced (1½ cups)
½	cup bacon drippings
½	medium white onion, chopped
1	medium green bell pepper, chopped
2	celery ribs, chopped
2	tsp. granulated garlic
2	Tbsp. sugar
1	tsp. dried crushed red pepper
2	tsp. salt

Hot cooked white rice
Garnish: ¼ cup chopped fresh flat-leaf parsley leaves

1. Place beans in a Dutch oven. Cover with water 2 inches above beans. Let soak 8 hours. Drain.
2. Brown sausage in bacon drippings in a 4-qt. saucepan. Remove sausage from pan. Add onion and next 2 ingredients to drippings in pan, and sauté over medium-high heat 2 minutes or until fragrant. Add beans and 6 cups water. Bring to a boil; reduce heat, and simmer, uncovered, stirring occasionally, 1 hour.
3. Add garlic, next 3 ingredients, and browned sausage, and cook for 20 more minutes to let flavors combine. Serve red beans over hot cooked rice. **Makes 10 servings.**

Lasyone's Bread Pudding

Instant vanilla pudding and rum combine for a quick sauce.

2	(13-oz.) packages hot dog buns
1	Tbsp. baking powder
6	cups milk, divided
1¾	cups sugar
2	Tbsp. butter, melted
⅛	tsp. ground cinnamon
1	(14-oz.) can sweetened condensed milk
8	large eggs
1	cup chopped pecans
1	(3.4-oz.) package vanilla instant pudding mix
2	tsp. butter
2	tsp. sugar
½	cup dark rum

1. Preheat oven to 350°. Tear hot dog buns into 1-inch pieces in a large bowl; toss with baking powder.
2. Whisk together 4 cups milk and next 5 ingredients; pour over buns, stirring to coat. (It should be a little soupy.) Fold in pecans. Pour into a lightly greased 13- x 9-inch baking dish.
3. Bake at 350° for 1 hour to 1 hour and 10 minutes or until puffed and golden brown.
4. While bread pudding bakes, prepare vanilla pudding mix with remaining 2 cups milk in a medium bowl according to package directions.
5. Combine ⅔ cup water, 2 tsp. butter, and 2 tsp. sugar in a small saucepan; cook over medium heat 3 minutes or until sugar dissolves. Remove from heat; stir into vanilla pudding. Stir in rum.
6. Remove bread pudding from oven; let stand 20 minutes before serving. Cut bread pudding into generous squares, and serve warm with rum sauce. **Makes 12 servings.**

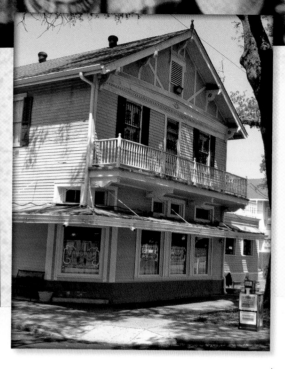

Mandina's Sazerac

Those in the know drink this Big Easy cocktail with a sniff and a sip. The lemon gives the exceptionally strong drink an especially clean aroma.

Dash of absinthe
Dash of Peychaud's aromatic cocktail bitters
    (more if you prefer a sweeter cocktail)
Dash of Angostura bitters
2   Tbsp. Simple Syrup (page 27)
¼   cup rye whiskey
Lemon rind strip or curl

1. Swirl absinthe in an ice-cold glass. (You want only to coat the glass with the absinthe, no more.) Add Peychaud's and Angostura bitters, followed by Simple Syrup and rye whiskey. Before garnishing the drink with lemon rind, rub it around the rim of the glass. **Makes 1 serving.**

Mandina's Restaurant

3800 Canal Street
New Orleans, Louisiana
(504) 482-9179

I showed up recently at Mandina's looking like I'd been hit by a streetcar named Bourbon. Fourth-generation owner Cindy Mandina didn't bat an eye. "Darlin', you need some hair of the dog," she said. "I'll have Marty make you a Sazerac." You have to love New Orleans, a town that serves the best hangover food on earth. Mandina's is my go-to spot for po'boys on perfect French bread, divine trout meunière, and turtle soup to dream about. And that Sazerac? Made in the grand tradition of New Orleans' signature cocktail, it starts with a swirl of absinthe in the glass. A stop at Mandina's cured my booze hangover but left me in a food coma. Ah, well. Laissez les bons temps rouler!

Mandina's "Turtle" Soup

Turtle being hard to come by, there is no turtle meat in this dish. It's no less indulgent with veal.

¾ cup butter
1 cup all-purpose flour
½ cup chopped onion
¼ cup chopped celery
¼ cup chopped green bell pepper
1 lb. boneless veal shoulder, cut in ¼-inch pieces
½ tsp. salt
8 cups beef broth
4 cups chicken broth
1 (28-oz.) can tomato puree
1 Tbsp. garlic powder
2½ tsp. dried thyme
2½ tsp. ground allspice
1 tsp. dried crushed red pepper
4 bay leaves
½ cup dry sherry
¼ cup minced fresh parsley
3 hard-cooked eggs, minced
2 tsp. sugar (optional)

1. Melt butter in a heavy 8-qt. stockpot or Dutch oven over medium heat; gradually whisk in flour, and cook, whisking constantly, 3 minutes or until flour is peanut butter colored. (Do not burn.)
2. Stir in onion, celery, and bell pepper; cook, stirring constantly, 3 minutes. Stir in veal and ½ tsp. salt; cook 1 minute. Gradually stir in broths; add tomato puree and next 5 ingredients. Bring to a boil; reduce heat, and simmer, stirring occasionally, 20 minutes or until veal is tender and soup is thick.
3. Stir in sherry, parsley, and eggs. Taste and add sugar, if needed, to balance acidity from tomato puree. Remove and discard bay leaves.
Makes about 1 gallon.

Mandina's

Picking a favorite restaurant in Louisiana is like being asked, "What's your favorite color?" Well, for teeth, it's white. I kinda prefer green trucks. It all depends. So Mandina's is my go-to spot when I'm about to leave the Big Easy. The happy pink facade and the gentle rumble of the streetcars outside never fail to make me smile. If there's one taste I want to remember from the city, it's Mandina's po'boys and turtle soup. Visiting here before I leave NOLA is like getting a good-bye hug at the airport—bittersweet but somehow reassuring that next time I return, this century-old restaurant will welcome me again with an unforgettable meal.

Rocky & Carlo's Restaurant & Bar

613 West Saint Bernard Highway
Chalmette, Louisiana
(504) 279-8323

The notice at the entrance reads, "Ladies Invited." They are indeed. But, truly, everyone feels welcome at Rocky & Carlo's. An institution here since a time when ladies weren't always welcome in bars, the restaurant was flooded by Hurricane Katrina and recently suffered a kitchen fire. But you can't keep a grand Italian family down. The Tommaseos and Gioes still run the place—and it's as fantastic as ever. The fare is simple Italian: hearty and delicious. I'm a huge fan of their Italian salad and veal parm, both of which are local favorites. And if you make it to the restaurant, don't miss their mac-and-cheese. You won't find better, but it's practically impossible for a home cook to reproduce. You'll just have to visit.

Rocky & Carlo's Italian Salad

*Tangy, salty, and nicely chopped, this very green
salad sports no tomatoes. Bet you won't miss them.*

5   cups chopped romaine lettuce
1   cup pimiento-stuffed Spanish olives
½   cup thinly sliced white onion
½   cup chopped celery
½   cup thinly sliced red cabbage
¼   cup chopped fresh parsley
3   garlic cloves, minced
Zesty Italian dressing
Grated Parmesan cheese

1. Toss together first 7 ingredients in a large bowl.
Serve with your favorite zesty Italian dressing and
plenty of Parmesan cheese. **Makes 4 servings.**

Rocky & Carlo's Veal Parmesan

Dense and cheesy, this is served with a very simple marinara sauce and the pasta of the day.

- 8   (2-oz.) veal cutlets
- 1   tsp. salt
- 1   tsp. freshly ground pepper
- ½   cup milk
- 3   large eggs
- 4   cups Italian-seasoned breadcrumbs
- ¼   cup unsalted butter
- ¼   cup olive oil
- 2   cups marinara sauce
- 1   cup grated Parmesan cheese
- 8   cups cooked spaghetti or other long pasta

Garnishes: chopped flat-leaf parsley, grated Parmesan cheese

1. Preheat oven to 350°. Place cutlets between 2 sheets of plastic wrap, and flatten to ⅛-inch thickness, using a rolling pin or flat side of a meat mallet. Sprinkle cutlets with salt and pepper.
2. Whisk together milk and eggs in a small bowl. Dip cutlets in egg mixture, and dredge in breadcrumbs, liberally coating all sides.
3. Melt 2 Tbsp. butter with 2 Tbsp. oil in a large heavy skillet over medium-high heat. Add half of cutlets; cook 2 minutes on each side or until golden brown. Transfer cutlets to a 13- x 9-inch baking dish; keep warm. Repeat procedure with remaining butter, oil, and cutlets.
4. Pour marinara sauce over cutlets, and sprinkle with Parmesan cheese. Bake at 350° for 20 minutes or until thoroughly heated. Serve over hot cooked pasta. **Makes 4 servings.**

OVERHEARD: "Laissez les bons temps rouler."
You'll hear this classic Louisiana expression most commonly during Mardi Gras or in the vicinity of New Orleans's Bourbon Street. It means, "Let the good times roll." And the good times roll in the Big Easy. Oh, yes, they do.

The Metro Diner ↗

Indian Pass
Raw Bar ↖

Weaver D's ↙

Boll Weevil Cafe
& Sweetery ↙

Chicken and
the Egg ↖

Frenchy's Cafe ↗

The Hil ↖

www.chickandtheegg.com

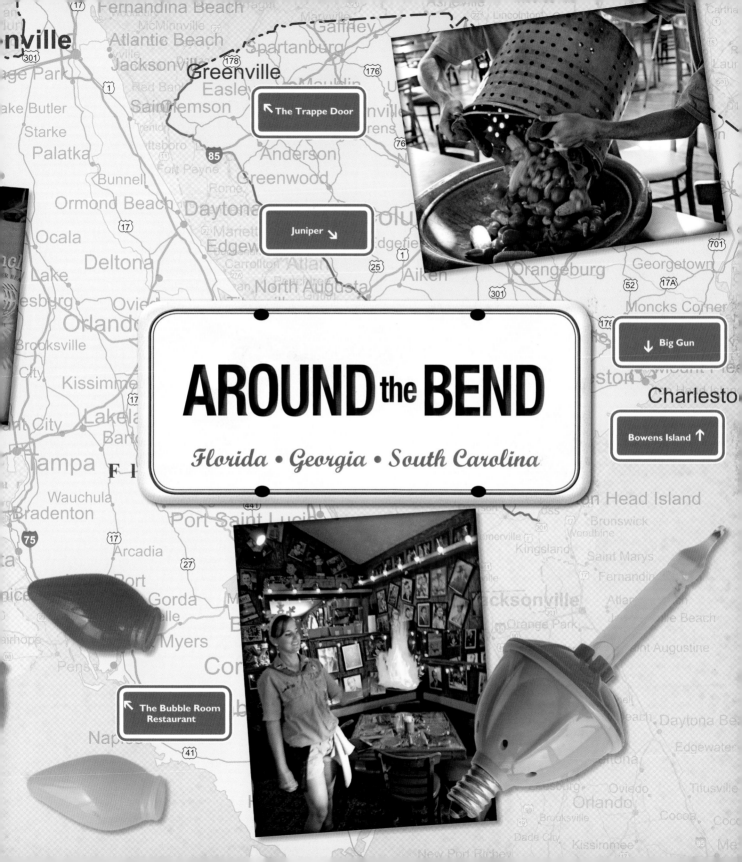

AROUND the BEND

Florida • Georgia • South Carolina

↑ The Trappe Door

Juniper →

↓ Big Gun

Bowens Island ↑

← The Bubble Room
Restaurant

Eddie Fisherman Grouper in a Bag

Named for entertainer Eddie Fisher, this sweet and nutty dish is the Bubble Room's oldest menu item and one of its most popular. The fish is baked in a paper lunch sack that's cut open at the table.

½   cup walnuts
10   round buttery crackers
¼   cup butter, softened
2   Tbsp. brown sugar
1   Tbsp. pineapple juice
4   (8-oz.) fresh grouper fillets
½   tsp. salt
½   tsp. freshly ground pepper
4   new brown paper lunch bags, dredged in vegetable oil

Garnish: lemon wedge, flat-leaf parsley sprigs

1. Preheat oven to 450°. Pulse walnuts in a food processor 6 times or until very fine. Add crackers; pulse until crushed and evenly mixed with walnuts. Transfer to a bowl; stir in butter, brown sugar, and pineapple juice until combined.

2. Sprinkle grouper fillets with salt and pepper. Spoon about 3 Tbsp. walnut mixture over each fillet; place 1 fillet in each bag. Fold the open edge of each bag over 5 times (this ensures that the grouper cooks without losing steam).

3. Place bags on a baking sheet. Bake at 450° for 15 minutes or just until fish flakes with a fork.

4. Transfer bags to serving plates using a spatula; cut open bags with scissors or a knife just before eating. **Makes 4 servings.**

Note: To prepare the lunch bags, pour vegetable oil to a depth of ½ inch in a shallow baking dish. Dip each bag into oil and lift up, allowing excess to drip off.

The Bubble Room Restaurant

15001 Captiva Drive
Captiva Island, Florida
(239) 472-5558

This wacky little beach dive feels animated, like some cartoon fairy tale of a restaurant. Toys, movie-star posters, vintage vending machines, and bubble lights festoon every square inch. Servers, known as "Bubble Scouts," will guide you through the extensive menu, which features everything from she-crab soup to roast duck. Portions are huge, and the dessert platter groans under the weight of eight cake varieties, including the delicious Red Velvet. The Bubble Room also boasts one of the best restaurant gift shops I've ever visited, filled with funny hats, Christmas lights, and colorful doodads.

Bubble Room Red Velvet Cake

This Elmo-red version is very moist and boasts chopped toasted pecans in the cream cheese frosting.

Cake

2½	cups self-rising soft-wheat flour
1½	cups sugar
1	tsp. baking soda
1	tsp. unsweetened cocoa
½	tsp. salt
2	large eggs
1½	cups vegetable oil
1	cup buttermilk
1	tsp. vanilla extract
1	tsp. white vinegar
2	(1-oz.) bottles red liquid food coloring

Frosting

1½	cups chopped pecans
10	oz. cream cheese, softened
1	cup butter, softened
1	(16-oz.) package powdered sugar

1. Prepare Cake: Preheat oven to 350°. Stir together first 5 ingredients in a large bowl. Whisk eggs in another large bowl. Whisk in oil and next 4 ingredients; gradually add to flour mixture, beating at low speed with an electric mixer until blended, stopping to scrape down sides as needed. Pour batter into 3 greased and floured 9-inch round cake pans.

2. Bake at 350° for 18 to 20 minutes or until a wooden pick inserted in center comes out clean. Cool in pans on wire racks 10 minutes; remove from pans to wire racks, and cool completely (about 1 hour).

3. Prepare Frosting: Preheat oven to 350°. Bake pecans in a single layer in a shallow pan 8 minutes or until toasted and fragrant, stirring halfway through. Let cool. Beat cream cheese and butter at medium speed with an electric mixer until smooth. Gradually add powdered sugar, beat at low speed just until combined. Beat at medium speed until smooth.

4. Frost top of first cake layer and sprinkle with ½ cup pecans. Add second cake layer; frost top, and sprinkle with ½ cup pecans. Add third cake layer and frost top and sides of cake. Lightly tap the frosting with the back of a spoon to create soft peaks all over the cake. Sprinkle top of cake with remaining ½ cup pecans. **Makes 10 to 12 servings.**

SOUNDTRACK:

"Orange Blossoms" by JJ Grey & Mofro

"If It's the Beaches" by the Avett Brothers

"Powder Your Face With Sunshine" by Dean Martin

"Cool Me Out" by The Embers

"All for You" by Florida natives Sister Hazel

"Hope You End Up With Me" by The Currys

Florida

Frenchy's Cafe

41 Baymont Street
Clearwater Beach, Florida
(727) 446-3607

If you wear anything more formal than flip-flops and a T-shirt to the original Frenchy's Cafe, you'll be dramatically overdressed. This Clearwater institution may seem simple—the menu staples are beer, shrimp, and grouper—but owner Mike "Frenchy" Preston, is a stickler for quality. A Quebec native whose menu includes classics like poutine (french fries with brown gravy and cheese curds), Frenchy has his own fleet of fishing boats to ensure that the catch is fresh even for the most basic of sandwiches. He serves up a mean seafood gumbo and also claims to have invented the Grouper Reuben. And, if you're lucky enough to see them on the menu, order the grouper cheeks. Yes, groupers have cheeks—and they are amazing.

Frenchy's Grouper Reubens

Originally a nod to the snowbird crowd, these tasty sandwiches are now a Florida staple. If you like, save two syllables, and call 'em Greubens.

4   (6-oz.) grouper fillets
1   tsp. garlic powder
1   tsp. paprika
2   Tbsp. olive oil
2   cups drained jarred refrigerated sauerkraut
8   marble rye bread slices
8   (1-oz.) Swiss cheese slices
½   cup Thousand Island dressing

1. Preheat oven to 425°. Sprinkle grouper fillets with garlic powder and paprika. Cook 2 grouper fillets in 1 Tbsp. hot oil in a large nonstick skillet over medium-high heat 3 to 4 minutes on each side or just until fish flakes with a fork. Remove from skillet; keep warm. Repeat procedure with remaining grouper fillets and oil.
2. Meanwhile, cook sauerkraut in a small saucepan over medium heat 3 minutes or until warm, stirring often.
3. Place bread slices on a baking sheet; bake at 425° for 2 minutes on each side or until toasted. Top bread with cheese, and bake 2 minutes more.
4. Layer 4 bread slices, cheese sides up, with sauerkraut, dressing, and grouper; top with remaining bread slices, cheese sides down.
Makes 4 servings.

Note: We tested with Bubbies Old Fashioned Sauerkraut, found in the refrigerated section.

Indian Pass
Raw Bar

8391 Indian Pass Road
Port St. Joe, Florida
(850) 227-1670

Where does a travel editor go to get away and relax? At the risk of making my favorite spot too popular, I'll admit: It's here. The Raw Bar sits right on 30-A, one of the greatest highways on the planet. The old painted sign and gracious front porch have had the same Panhandle ramshackle look, comfortable and worn, for generations. Time is a bit mysterious here: Nobody is sure whether the Raw Bar is on Central or Eastern Time, but really, who cares? Early, late, whatever. Just kick back with a beer from the enormous fridge (the honor system applies), and order up some of the South's best oysters. I highly recommend scarfing your Apalachicola bivalves raw (it is the "Raw Bar" after all), downing a half-dozen

Indian Pass Oysters

It doesn't get any simpler, or easier, than this.

As many shucked fresh oysters as you please
As many cold beers as you please

1. Slurp. Sip. Repeat. (Told you it was easy!)
Makes the perfect amount.

Blue Moon beers, and dancing with your sweetheart late into a Florida summer night. Can't make it to the Emerald Coast? No problem. The Raw Bar's head honcho, Jimmy McNeill, gave me every recipe the joint offers. That took 90 seconds and, reading back over them, I think I may have been drinking at the time. Oh well, that's the Raw Bar way—a little vague, very casual, and always ready to host another beach-bound diner.

OVERHEARD: "We boil 'em with their britches on!"

"Jimmy Mac," owner of the Indian Pass Raw Bar, is about the most colorful character in the Panhandle. He said this when I asked if he peeled the shrimp at the Raw Bar before cooking them.

Indian Pass
Steamed Shrimp

If you can simmer water, you can make these.

Old Bay seasoning
Cajun seasoning
A mess of unpeeled shrimp

1. Sprinkle seasonings on your shrimp. Place in a steamer basket over simmering water. Steam until shrimp are pink (4 to 6 minutes, depending on their size). **Makes the perfect amount.**

Indian Pass Raw Bar

Let me share this fantasy of mine. No, not the one about Facebook inventing a "Shhh!" button. The one about me, a pretty blonde, and this little beach hangout. The bombshell and I have been enjoying the crystal blue water all day. The sparkling white beach feels warm (but not so hot you have to run saying, "Eww! Ha! Cha! HAH!") Her tan looks as magnificent as my abs, and after reading Peggy Noonan's column in *The Wall Street Journal*, (hey, this is MY fantasy), she says something like, "Hey, babe, let's go have some oysters and beer." The joint—creaky and weathered— brims with characters who have been known to blow in their own pickup's door with dynamite (ask them to show you the YouTube video). Groovy musicians play songs, and the pretty lass and I dance the night away. The beer never gets warm, the oysters are the best on earth, and the host knows my name. The place? Indian Pass Raw Bar. The good news? It really does exist.

The Metro Diner

3302 Hendricks Avenue
Jacksonville, Florida
(904) 398-3701

I can't breathe. I can barely feel my face. I think I have eaten enough calories to feed a small village. Listen to me here: They were all worth it. This little diner, which is always packed with locals, serves up incredibly inventive food. But it is not some place you want to go if you're a bikini model. They serve something called the Vortex— a delicious burger with house-smoked bacon and slaw, sandwiched between TWO grilled cheese sandwiches (the caloric equivalent of a nuclear weapon). And then there's the Yo Hala—a gooey French toast stuffed with cream cheese and banana slices. It's one of my all-time favorite desserts, and though it's roughly the size of a Buick, I ate all of mine and half of head chef Mark Davoli's. I hate him; he's my new best friend.

Metro Diner's Huevos Rancheros

I normally wouldn't eat these in Florida, but man, they are awesome. The crumbly Spanish-style chorizo and fresh flour tortilla chips make all the difference.

2   large green bell peppers, cut into strips
1   large onion, cut into ¼-inch-thick slices
1   lb. fresh chorizo sausage, casings removed
3   (15-oz.) cans black beans, drained and rinsed
2   (10-inch) flour tortillas
Vegetable oil
1   cup (4 oz.) shredded Cheddar cheese
1   cup (4 oz.) shredded mozzarella cheese
8   large eggs
Toppings: salsa, sour cream, pickled jalapeño
     pepper slices

1. Preheat oven to 300°. Heat a grill pan over medium-high heat; cook bell pepper strips and onion slices 2 to 3 minutes on each side or until tender, and marked by grill.
2. Meanwhile, brown sausage in a large skillet over medium-high heat, stirring often, 5 minutes or until sausage crumbles and is no longer pink; drain and return to skillet. Stir in bell peppers, onion, and beans. Cover and keep warm.
3. Cut each tortilla into 8 wedges. Pour oil to depth of 1½ inches in a large heavy skillet; heat to 350°. Fry tortilla wedges, in batches, 1 to 2 minutes or until golden brown. Drain on paper towels.
4. Place tortilla chips, points out, in a lightly greased 13- x 9-inch baking dish. Scatter chorizo sausage mixture over tortilla chips; sprinkle with cheeses. Bake at 300° for 10 minutes or until cheeses melt.

5. Meanwhile, heat a large nonstick skillet over medium heat. Coat with vegetable oil. Gently break 3 eggs into hot skillet. Cook 2 to 3 minutes on each side or to desired degree of doneness.

Repeat procedure with remaining eggs. Place eggs on top of chorizo sausage mixture. Top with salsa, sour cream, and pickled jalapeño pepper slices. **Makes 8 servings.**

Metro Diner's Strawberry Butter

This sweet and fruity pink butter is perfect on biscuits, waffles, pancakes, or toast.

1 cup butter, softened
3 Tbsp. powdered sugar
2 Tbsp. grenadine
¼ cup finely chopped strawberries

1. Beat butter at high speed with an electric mixer 3 minutes or until creamy. Add powdered sugar and grenadine; beat until blended. Stir in strawberries. Cover and chill 30 minutes. **Makes 1½ cups.**

Metro Diner's Yo Hala

The name's a riff on Challah (the "c" is silent), the eggy bread with which this is made. Easily among one of the top five desserts I've ever eaten, it's a towering stack of stuffed French toast goodness. I think it should be called Challah Back. Any leftover Berry Compote makes a delicious addition to a bowl of vanilla ice cream or a slice of pound cake.

Filling

2 (8-oz.) packages cream cheese, softened
½ cup firmly package light brown sugar
2 Tbsp. hazelnut liqueur
4 bananas, cut into ½-inch-thick slices (4½ cups sliced)

Berry Compote

1 (10-oz.) package frozen whole strawberries, thawed
1½ pt. fresh blueberries
½ cup firmly packed light brown sugar
½ tsp. fresh lemon juice
2 tsp. cornstarch

French Toast

6 large eggs
½ cup milk
2 Tbsp. sugar
2 tsp. vanilla extract
½ tsp. ground cinnamon
8 (1-inch-thick) slices challah bread
2 Tbsp. butter
Powdered sugar

1. **Prepare Filling:** Beat cream cheese and sugar at medium speed with an electric mixer until smooth. Stir in hazelnut liqueur. Fold in bananas. Cover and chill 1 hour.

2. **Prepare Berry Compote:** Cut large strawberries in half. Combine ¾ cup water, blueberries, brown sugar, and lemon juice in a medium

saucepan; bring to a boil, stirring occasionally. Combine cornstarch and 1 Tbsp. cold water, stirring until smooth. Stir cornstarch mixture into berries; cook, stirring constantly, 1 minute or until thickened. Stir in strawberries. Remove from heat; keep warm.

3. Prepare French Toast: Whisk eggs in a large shallow dish. Whisk in milk and next 3 ingredients. Spread ½ cup Filling on each of 4 challah bread slices; top with remaining bread slices. Cut diagonally in half; dredge sandwich halves in egg mixture, shaking off excess.

4. Melt 1 Tbsp. butter in a large skillet over medium-high heat. Add 4 sandwich halves; cook 1 to 2 minutes on all sides (including edges) or until golden brown. Remove from skillet; keep warm. Repeat procedure with remaining butter and sandwich halves. Serve with Berry Compote; dust with powdered sugar. **Makes 4 servings.**

Boll Weevil Jambalaya

¼   cup butter, divided
1   lb. skinned and boned chicken breast, diced
1   lb. andouille sausage, chopped
¾   cup diced red bell pepper
¾   cup diced green bell pepper
1   cup diced onion
½   cup diced celery
½   lb. ham, diced
1   (14.5-oz.) can diced tomatoes, drained
½   cup dry white wine
⅓   cup tomato paste
2   tsp. seasoned salt
2   tsp. Cajun blackened seasoning
1   tsp. ground red pepper
1   cup heavy cream
¾   lb. unpeeled, medium-size raw shrimp
1   tsp. Cajun blackened seasoning
6   cups cooked long-grain rice

1. Melt 2 Tbsp. butter in a Dutch oven over medium-high heat. Add chicken and sausage; sauté 5 minutes. Add bell peppers, onion, and celery; sauté 5 minutes.
2. Add 1 cup water, ham, and next 6 ingredients; simmer, uncovered, 30 minutes. Add cream; simmer 15 more minutes.
3. Peel shrimp; devein, if desired. Sprinkle shrimp with blackened seasoning.
4. Melt remaining 2 Tbsp. butter in a large skillet over medium-high heat. Add shrimp; sauté 3 minutes or just until shrimp turn pink. Serve jambalaya over rice; top with shrimp. **Makes 8 servings.**

Boll Weevil Cafe & Sweetery

10 Ninth Street/James Brown Boulevard
Augusta, Georgia
(706) 722-7772

The Boll Weevil started as a place for guys to get together, drink, and play cards. If that isn't a recipe for success, I don't know what is. From those humble beginnings, the Boll Weevil grew to a phenomenal bakery and restaurant. You'll want to try their José, a spicy sandwich stuffed with jalapeños and made with the bakery's own honey-wheat bread. It's a hot-sweet treat that can't be beat. I'm also a fan of the jambalaya.

Chicken and the Egg

800 Whitlock Avenue, Suite 124
Marietta, Georgia
(678) 388-8813

You might think you'd find Atlanta's most chichi Southern fare only in its bustling downtown. You'd be wrong. Dixie dishes like ice-cream floats and fried green tomatoes are works of art at chef Marc Taft's restaurant on the suburban outskirts. This spacious eatery in an upscale strip mall may initially seem too slick to be close to the farms and farmers supplying its sustainable menu. But dig into one of these dishes, and you will immediately taste the restaurant's commitment to local, fresh, and organic. It's a passion for Marc and his wife, Elizabeth, and one that will make you feel good about eating their farmstead fare.

Chicken and the Egg's Fried Green Tomatoes

This is fancy-pants dinner-party good: tangy fried tomato in a pool of salty cheese goodness with little flakes of country ham and dabs of sweet tomato jam. It's also a recipe with several steps and an overnight soak. So be sure to start a day ahead.

Fried Green Tomatoes (page 174)
½   cup Tomato Jam (page 174)
Pimiento Cheese Fondue (page 175)
¼   cup chopped thinly sliced country ham
Garnish: fresh thyme leaves

1. Prepare Fried Green Tomatoes through Step 2. Prepare Tomato Jam as directed.
2. After green tomato slices have soaked 24 hours and up to 1 hour before serving time, complete Fried Green Tomatoes as directed. Keep warm in a 200° oven.
3. Prepare Pimiento Cheese Fondue as directed. Pour or spoon Pimiento Cheese Fondue onto a rectangular platter. Shingle fried tomato slices down the plate, alternating sides so they are left and right of center. Top each tomato slice with a tablespoon of Tomato Jam. Sprinkle country ham down center of plate. Serve immediately. **Makes 4 to 8 servings.**

CHICKEN AND THE EGG

MODERN FARMSTEAD FARE

Fried Green Tomatoes

2   green tomatoes, each cut into 4
      (¼-inch-thick) slices
½   tsp. kosher salt
2   cups buttermilk
½   tsp. hot sauce
1¼   cups all-purpose soft-wheat flour
½   cup plain yellow cornmeal
1   Tbsp. freshly ground pepper
1   Tbsp. kosher salt
Vegetable oil

1. Arrange tomato slices in a single layer on a baking sheet; sprinkle with ½ tsp. salt. Let tomato slices stand 1 hour.

2. Rinse tomato slices with cold water; drain. Place tomato slices in a large, shallow container. Combine buttermilk and hot sauce; pour over tomatoes. Cover and chill 24 hours.

3. Stir together flour and next 3 ingredients in a large shallow bowl.

4. Pour oil to depth of 1 inch in a 12-inch cast-iron skillet; heat to 350°. Remove tomato slices from buttermilk mixture, reserving buttermilk mixture. Working in batches, dredge tomato slices in flour mixture; shake off excess. Dip tomato slices back in buttermilk mixture, and dredge again in flour mixture; shake off excess.

5. Fry tomatoes, in batches, 2 minutes on each side or until golden brown. Drain on a wire rack in a jelly-roll pan. **Makes 8 slices.**

Tomato Jam

This makes a little more than you'll need for this recipe, but it's so tasty that that's a very good thing. Enjoy leftovers with goat cheese and crackers or tucked into a gourmet grilled cheese.

¼   cup finely chopped Vidalia onion
Pinch of kosher salt
2   Tbsp. olive oil
¼   cup grated fresh ginger
3   garlic cloves, minced
1   tsp. ground coriander
1   tsp. ground cinnamon
½   tsp. ground cumin
⅛   tsp. ground cloves
⅛   tsp. ground allspice
⅛   tsp. ground red pepper
3¼   cups chopped seeded peeled tomatoes (2½ lb.)
½   cup firmly packed light brown sugar
¼   cup sherry vinegar
¼   cup honey
1   tsp. kosher salt
½   tsp. freshly ground pepper
2   Tbsp. fresh lemon juice

1. Sauté onion and pinch of salt in hot oil in a large skillet over medium-high heat 1 to 2 minutes or until tender. Add ginger and garlic; sauté 1 minute. Stir in coriander, cinnamon, cumin, cloves, allspice, and ground red pepper; sauté 30 seconds. Stir in tomatoes, brown sugar, and vinegar. Bring to a boil; reduce heat, and simmer, stirring often, 18 minutes or until tomatoes break down and almost all the liquid evaporates. Stir in honey, 1 tsp. salt, and freshly ground pepper. Bring to a boil, and cook 2 minutes or until mixture is silky and thick.

2. Remove from heat. Stir in lemon juice; let cool completely (about 45 minutes). Cover and store in refrigerator up to 1 week. **Makes 2¼ cups.**

Pimiento Cheese Fondue

½   cup (2 oz.) shredded white Cheddar cheese
¼   cup (1 oz.) shredded sharp Cheddar cheese
⅓   cup mayonnaise
2   Tbsp. chopped roasted red bell pepper
Pinch of kosher salt
Dash of hot sauce
Pinch of ground red pepper
1   oz. cream cheese, diced
½   cup heavy cream

1. Stir together first 7 ingredients in a small saucepan. Add cream cheese, pressing into the mixture with the back of a spoon to ensure no large chunks are left. Stir in cream; cook over medium-low heat, stirring constantly, 12 minutes or until cheese is melted and smooth. Serve immediately. **Makes 1¼ cups.**

Chicken and the Egg

For many years, I performed my reserve Navy drill duty each month at the nearby Dobbins Air Force Base. (Yeah, yeah, I know. "What's the Navy doing in Atlanta?" you ask. It's called irony. Sorta like a sailor being sent to war in landlocked Afghanistan. But I digress.) Anyway, I searched Marietta for a great place for years. Like, scoured the town and shook old ladies on street corners: "You MUST tell me where I can find good food!" Nothing. Zilch. Zero. Then, like a lighthouse in a squall, Chicken and the Egg appeared. It has an organic menu. An inventive chef. A bar you could land a plane on. A gorgeous dining room. Hallelujah! And then I was transferred to the Pentagon. Typical.

Chicken and the Egg's "Cherry Cola Float" Chocolate Cake à la Mode

This innovative twist on a Southern classic is one to enjoy with a fork rather than a straw.

Cherry-Cola Compote (next page)
Cola Swirl Ice Cream (next page)
Parchment paper
Vegetable cooking spray
1¼ cups sugar
½ cup butter, softened
1½ cups all-purpose soft-wheat flour
3 Tbsp. unsweetened cocoa
½ tsp. baking soda
¼ tsp. salt
1 large egg
¾ cup cola soft drink
½ cup buttermilk
1 tsp. vanilla extract
Garnish: sugar-dipped fresh cherries

1. Prepare Cherry-Cola Compote through Step 1. Prepare Cola Swirl Ice Cream as directed.
2. Preheat oven to 350°. Line bottom of a lightly greased 13- x 9-inch pan with parchment paper; lightly coat parchment paper with cooking spray.
3. Beat sugar and butter at medium speed with an electric mixer until creamy. Whisk together flour and next 3 ingredients in a medium bowl. Whisk together egg and next 3 ingredients in another medium bowl. Add flour mixture to butter mixture alternately with egg mixture, beginning and ending with flour mixture. Beat at low speed until blended after each addition, stopping to scrape bowl as needed.
4. Pour batter into prepared pan. Bake at 350° for 25 minutes or until a wooden pick inserted in center comes out clean. Cool completely in pan on wire rack (about 30 minutes).
5. Meanwhile, complete Cherry-Cola Compote. Cut cooled cake into 12 squares.
6. To serve, spoon about ¼ cup Cherry-Cola Compote onto a plate; top with a piece of cake. Place a ¼-cup scoop of Cola Swirl Ice Cream on top of cake, and more compote, if desired. **Makes 12 servings.**

Cherry-Cola Compote

2   lb. fresh cherries, pitted and divided
2   cups cola soft drink
1½ cups sugar

1. Cut one-third of cherries in half. Combine halved cherries and cola soft drink in a bowl. Cover and chill 8 to 24 hours.
2. Stir together remaining two-thirds of cherries, sugar, and ½ cup water in a large saucepan over medium-high heat, and cook, stirring occasionally, 20 minutes or until cherries have softened. Fill a large bowl with ice. Place bowl containing cherry mixture in ice, and let stand, stirring occasionally, 30 minutes or until cooled. Process cooled cherry mixture in a food processor until smooth, stopping to scrape down sides as needed.
3. Drain cherry halves, discarding cola. Stir together cherry halves and pureed cherry mixture in a medium bowl. **Makes 4 cups.**

Cola Swirl Ice Cream

For a shortcut, make the cola syrup and fold it into a softened quart of ready-made vanilla ice cream.

1½ cups cola soft drink
1   cup milk
2   cups heavy cream, divided
¾   cup sugar, divided
Pinch of salt
6   egg yolks

1. Bring cola soft drink to a boil in a small saucepan; reduce heat to medium, and simmer until reduced by half (about 32 minutes). Remove from heat, and cool completely (about 2 hours).
2. Combine milk, 1 cup cream, 6 Tbsp. sugar, and salt in a large heavy saucepan; bring to a boil, stirring constantly to dissolve sugar. Remove from heat.
3. Whisk together remaining 6 Tbsp. sugar and egg yolks. Gradually stir about half of hot milk mixture into yolk mixture; add yolk mixture to remaining hot milk mixture, stirring constantly. Cook over medium-low heat, stirring constantly and scraping the bottom, 5 minutes or until thick enough to coat the back of a spoon. (Don't let mixture boil.)
4. Strain mixture through a fine wire-mesh strainer into a metal bowl. Stir remaining 1 cup cream into strained mixture; let cool 1 hour. Cover and chill 2 hours and 45 minutes. Pour mixture into freezer container of a 1½-qt. electric ice-cream maker, and freeze according to manufacturer's instructions. (Instructions and times may vary.)
5. Fold cooled cola syrup into soft-frozen ice cream. Freeze in an airtight container 12 hours or until firm. **Makes 3⅓ cups.**

Coke®

www.chickandtheegg.com

The Hil

9110 Selborne Lane
Palmetto, Georgia
(770) 463-6040

Pull up a stool at The Hil's rustic-chic bar and order a Farm Dirty Martini or another of bartender Jim White's inventive cocktails. Then settle in for a delicious supper. The dining room wows with lovely views, fine linens, and a slightly European feel. It's not too swanky, though. Butcher paper covers the tables, and humble Mason jars (filled with house-made pickles and preserves) abound. The Hil is a mere 45 minutes from downtown Atlanta but feels worlds away. Chef Hilary White makes a mean chicken pot pie and award-winning Vidalia fritters. The Culinary Institute of America-trained chef insists on using farm-fresh produce, and one glance at her magnificent kitchen shows even the most casual diner that she's a stickler for quality and precision.

The Hil's Caramelized Vidalia Onion Fritters

These creamy-in-the-middle fritters have intense sweet-onion flavor, and they're delicious with a forkful of the flavorful slaw. Hakurei turnips are sweet, juicy Japanese salad turnips. They are worth seeking out at farmers' markets, but you can substitute daikon radish if you can't find them.

Vinaigrette

2½ Tbsp. white balsamic vinegar
2   tsp. brown sugar
2   tsp. stone-ground mustard
½   tsp. salt
½   tsp. minced garlic
¼   tsp. freshly ground pepper
2½ Tbsp. canola oil
2½ Tbsp. olive oil

Slaw

2   cups thinly sliced hakurei turnips
    or daikon radishes
1   cup thinly sliced radishes
¾   cup thinly sliced carrots
½   cup thinly sliced celery
⅓   cup thinly sliced Vidalia onion
¼   cup English peas

Fritters

6   cups diced Vidalia onions (4 large)
¼   cup canola oil
2   Tbsp. butter
½   cup (2 oz.) shredded Gouda cheese
¼   cup cooked and finely crumbled
    hickory-smoked bacon slices
¼   cup mayonnaise
1   tsp. salt
2   tsp. Dijon mustard
½   tsp. freshly ground pepper

Canola oil

1   cup all-purpose flour
1   cup milk
1   large egg
1   cup fine, dry breadcrumbs
½   cup panko (Japanese breadcrumbs)
Garnishes: pea shoots or watercress, celery leaves,
    minced fresh chives

1. Prepare Vinaigrette: Whisk together first
6 ingredients in a small bowl. Add oils in a slow,
steady stream, whisking constantly until smooth.
2. Prepare Slaw: Toss together all ingredients in
a medium bowl. Drizzle with vinaigrette, tossing
to coat. Cover and chill 1 hour.
3. Prepare Fritters: Place onions in ¼ cup hot
canola oil in a large skillet over medium heat, and
cook, stirring often, 25 minutes or until onions
are caramel colored. Stir in butter. Add 1 Tbsp.
water, stirring to loosen particles from bottom of
skillet. Stir together caramelized onions, Gouda
cheese, and next 5 ingredients in a large bowl.
Cover and freeze 20 minutes or until cold.
4. Pour canola oil to depth of 1½ inches into a
Dutch oven; heat to 350°. Place flour in a shallow
bowl. Whisk together milk and egg in a second
shallow bowl. Stir together breadcrumbs and
panko in a third shallow bowl. Shape chilled
onion mixture into balls using a 1½-inch-diameter
cookie-dough scoop. Dredge each ball in flour,
dip in milk mixture, and dredge in breadcrumb
mixture, coating well and shaking off excess
between each step. Fry fritters, in batches,
1 minute or until golden brown. Drain on a
wire rack over paper towels.
5. To serve, divide slaw among salad plates; top
with fritters. **Makes 10 servings.**

OVERHEARD: "I'm loster than an Easter egg in July."

Georgia is full of back roads, once you get off the mega-highways around Atlanta. And
yes, while headed to dinner at The Hil, I did finally admit to my pretty copilot that I
was, err, temporarily unsure of our whereabouts. I did NOT stop for directions.

Weaver D's

1016 East Broad Street
Athens, Georgia
(706) 353-7797

You can't miss the bright green building.
Or owner Dexter Weaver's bald head. Or
his signature statement: "automatic for
the people," which Dexter often shortens
to just "automatic" and delivers in a flat
monotone. (Fun fact: The phrase was
the inspiration for the R.E.M. album
Automatic for the People.) That, friend,
is called character, and Weaver D's has
character in ample supply, along with
Southern soul-food staples such as
collard greens and fried chicken. Go on,
stuff yourself silly. Because Athens is
a college town, the price tag is reasonable too. Best part? Overhearing Dexter
holler things like, "Loretta, get me some
green beans and some muffins. Got a
church group coming, mmm-hmmm!"

Weaver D's Squash Casserole

Creamy and simple, this tastes like the sort
grandmama used to make.

4	lb. yellow squash, cut into ¼-inch slices (14 cups sliced)
¼	cup butter
1¼	cups diced white onion
⅔	cup cream of mushroom soup
1	tsp. salt
1	tsp. garlic salt
½	tsp. pepper
2	large eggs, lightly beaten
1	cup soft, fresh breadcrumbs
1	cup (4 oz.) shredded sharp Cheddar cheese

1. Preheat oven to 350°. Cook squash in boiling water to cover 8 minutes or until tender. Drain well, and press gently between paper towels to remove excess moisture.
2. Melt butter in a large skillet over medium-high heat; add onion, and sauté 3 to 5 minutes or until tender.
3. Stir together onion mixture, soup, and next 4 ingredients in a large bowl. Stir in squash and breadcrumbs. Spoon mixture into a lightly greased 13- x 9-inch baking dish. Sprinkle with cheese, and bake at 350° for 30 minutes or until lightly browned. **Makes 12 servings.**

Weaver D's Buttermilk Cornbread Muffins

Serve these moist muffins warm and with plenty of butter. They bake best in heavy-duty (heavier weight) muffin pans. Leftovers freeze well when sealed tightly in a zip-top plastic freezer bag.

¼	cup vegetable oil
3	cups self-rising white cornmeal mix
¼	cup sugar
2	cups buttermilk
½	cup butter, melted
1	Tbsp. mayonnaise
3	large eggs, lightly beaten

1. Preheat oven to 425°. Spoon ½ tsp. vegetable oil into each of 24 standard muffin cups. Heat muffins pans in oven 5 minutes.

2. Combine cornmeal mix and sugar in a large bowl; make a well in center of mixture. Stir together buttermilk and remaining ingredients; add to cornmeal mixture, stirring just until dry ingredients are moistened. Spoon batter into hot muffin pans, filling two-thirds full.

3. Bake at 425° for 15 minutes or until golden brown. Remove from oven; tip muffins on their sides in the pan, using a knife. Serve warm.

Makes 2 dozen.

SOUNDTRACK:

"Burn the Honeysuckle" by the Gourds

"Night Time Is The Right Time" by Ray Charles

"Walking Down" by Joe Purdy

"Shiny Happy People" by R.E.M.

"Midnight Train to Georgia" by Gladys Knight & The Pips

"Blue Jeans" by Peach State adopted daughter Jessie James

"Georgia on My Mind" by Michael Bublé

WEAVER D'S
FINE F
"AUTOMATIC FOR THE PEOPLE"

Big Gun

137 Calhoun Street
Charleston, South Carolina
(843) 789-3821

Scratch beneath Charleston's formal and preppy surface, and you'll discover the Holy City's more casual underpinnings. Big Gun is the sort of hipster bar and live-music venue you might expect to find in San Francisco or on New York's Lower East side. Its menu goes beyond typical bar fare. Sure, you can get a burger and fries, but opt instead for owner Austin Kirkland's rich duck burger and Brussels sprouts. Or try the ultimate comfort food, the peppery and delicious Pee Dee chicken bog. It's named for the boggy Pee Dee River region of South Carolina. As you might expect from a big gun, it will blow you away.

Big Gun's Veggie Burgers

These are among the best veggie burgers I've ever had.

⅓	cup finely chopped onion
¼	cup finely chopped red bell pepper
3	Tbsp. minced garlic
2	Tbsp. diced canned artichoke hearts
2	tsp. seeded and minced jalapeño pepper
6	Tbsp. olive oil, divided
4	cups uncooked regular oats
1	cup drained and rinsed canned black-eyed peas
1	cup drained and rinsed canned green peas
1	cup drained and rinsed canned navy beans
¼	cup panko (Japanese breadcrumbs)
2	Tbsp. minced fresh parsley
1	Tbsp. hot sauce
2	tsp. dried oregano
1	tsp. dried thyme
1	tsp. paprika
1	tsp. celery salt
1	tsp. chili powder
1	tsp. ground cumin
1	tsp. dried crushed red pepper
2	large eggs, lightly beaten
8	hamburger buns, toasted

Toppings: mayonnaise mixed with Asian Sriracha hot chili sauce, flash-fried kale, tomato slices

1. Sauté first 5 ingredients in 2 Tbsp. hot oil in a large skillet over medium heat for 4 minutes or until onion is translucent. Transfer to large bowl; let cool 10 minutes. Add oats and next 14 ingredients, stirring until well blended.
2. Shape mixture into 8 (3¼-inch) patties. Cover and chill 30 minutes or until firm.
3. Cook patties, in 2 batches, in 2 Tbsp. hot oil (per batch) 4 minutes on each side.
4. Serve on toasted buns with desired toppings.
Makes 8 servings.

Big Gun's Pee Dee Chicken Bog

A chicken bog is a moist rice casserole-like dish prepared on the stove-top rather than in the oven and usually with homemade chicken broth, boiled chicken, and spicy sausage. It's a signature comfort food in South Carolina.

1	(4½- to 5-lb.) whole chicken
2	celery ribs, coarsely chopped
2	yellow onions, quartered
1	carrot, coarsely chopped
3	garlic cloves, halved
16	thyme sprigs
1	rosemary sprig
1	bay leaf
4	links hot Italian sausage (1 lb.)
2	Tbsp. canola oil, divided
½	cup butter, divided
1½	cups finely chopped onion
¾	cup finely chopped carrot
⅔	cup diced celery
3	garlic cloves, minced
½	cup dry white wine
2	Tbsp. hot sauce
¾	tsp. coarse sea salt
½	tsp. freshly ground pepper
2	cups uncooked extra-long-grain rice (such as Carolina Gold or Mahatma Gold)

1. Remove giblets and neck, if included, from chicken; reserve for another use. Place chicken, breast side up, and next 7 ingredients in an 8-qt. stockpot; add water to 1 inch above chicken.

2. Bring to a boil over high heat; reduce heat, and simmer, partially covered, 4 hours. Remove chicken from liquid, reserving liquid, and cool slightly (about 20 minutes).

3. While chicken and stock cool, cook sausage links in 1 Tbsp. hot oil in a large skillet over medium-low heat for 6 to 8 minutes or until sausage is browned and no longer pink in center. Cool slightly, and cut sausage links diagonally into thin slices.

4. Pour stock through a fine wire-mesh strainer into a bowl; discard solids. Let stock stand 10 minutes; skim fat from surface of stock. Reserve 4½ cups stock.

5. Remove meat from chicken, and shred into large chunks using two forks. Discard skin and bones.

6. Wipe Dutch oven clean. Melt ¼ cup butter with remaining 1 Tbsp. oil in Dutch oven; add 1½ cups onion, ¾ cup carrot, and ⅔ cup celery; sauté 3 minutes. Add minced garlic; sauté 1 minute. Add wine, and cook 2 minutes. Add reserved 4½ cups stock, hot sauce, salt, and pepper; bring to boil. Stir in rice; bring to a boil. Cover, reduce heat, and simmer 15 to 20 minutes or until rice is tender and liquid is absorbed. (The bog should still be moist.)

7. Remove from heat, and let stand 10 minutes. Stir in remaining ¼ cup butter, sliced sausage and pulled chicken. Season with additional hot sauce or pepper, if desired. (Traditionally, this dish is quite peppery.) **Makes 8 servings.**

Bowens Island

1870 Bowens Island Road
Charleston, South Carolina
(843) 795-2757

In the winding tributaries behind Folly Beach, you'll find one of my favorite hangouts in the South: Bowens Island. Bounce down the old dirt road, climb the ramp onto what's essentially a huge porch, and kick back with a cold beer and a bowl of Frogmore Stew. Then watch the sun sink into the marsh. I promise you: There's not a better moment. When the old jukebox plays a tune, grab your gal or fella and take a turn. Nobody will judge. It's the charm of Bowens Island, where generations of Carolinians have enjoyed the rustic, non-air-conditioned escape. Here the food is simple, life moves slowly, and the memories are guaranteed to linger.

Bowens Island Lump Crab Cakes

Moist, salty, and fantastic, these rival anything from Maryland.

1	lb. fresh jumbo lump crabmeat, drained
½	cup mayonnaise
1	Tbsp. Dijon mustard
1	Tbsp. Worcestershire sauce
1	Tbsp. hot sauce
Dash of freshly ground pepper	
1	large egg
2¾	cups coarsely crushed saltine crackers (24 crackers)
2	Tbsp. canola oil

1. Pick crabmeat, removing any bits of shell.

2. Whisk together mayonnaise and next 5 ingredients in a large bowl. Gently fold in crackers and crabmeat. Shape mixture into 6 (3-inch) patties. Cover and chill 1 hour or until firm.

3. Cook 3 patties in 1 Tbsp. hot oil in a large cast-iron skillet over medium-high heat 3 minutes on each side or until golden brown. Remove from skillet; keep warm. Repeat procedure with remaining 1 Tbsp. oil and patties. **Makes 6 servings.**

OVERHEARD: "It's hotter than blue blazes!"

Blue flames burn hotter than red or orange, so this expression means it's really hot out. When I was in Columbia, I complained about the heat to my elderly grandfather (who had been stationed at Fort Jackson in 1941). His reply: "Son, you know the only thing that separates Columbia from hell in the summertime is a screened door."

Bowens Island Frogmore Stew

This Lowcountry classic contains no frogs and isn't really a stew. Instead, it's a tasty boil (named for a coastal town you won't find on a map) and just perfect for a backyard get-together.

½ cup Old Bay seasoning
1 Tbsp. hot sauce
1 medium onion, peeled and quartered
1½ lb. new potatoes or baby red potatoes
1½ lb. smoked sausage, cut diagonally into ½-inch slices
6 ears fresh corn, halved
2 lb. unpeeled, large raw shrimp

1. Bring 3 quarts water, Old Bay seasoning, hot sauce, and onion to a boil in a large covered stockpot. Add potatoes, and cook, uncovered, 10 minutes. Add sausage and corn; return to a boil. Cook, uncovered, 10 minutes. Stir in shrimp. Cover; remove from heat, and let stand 10 minutes or just until shrimp turn pink. Drain. **Makes 10 servings.**

Note: The key to good Frogmore Stew is not overcooking the shrimp. Because there is a lot of heat in the potatoes, corn, and sausage, the shrimp will continue to cook a little even after you drain the stew.

Bowens Island

OK, you know the part in the movie when, on the eve of leaving to fight for all that's right and decent and good, our hero is at the PERFECT bar with his buddies? Yeah, that part. It should be filmed here. Bowens Island has all the right set pieces: gorgeous sunsets, a rustic bar, awesome food, and the only pretty girls on earth to whom you can say, "Hey, want to shag?" when you first meet them and not have your face slapped into the next county. (That line is almost as good as my other fave, "Hey, did we go to different schools together?") Anyway, make your own life's movie scene by visiting here at least once.

Juniper

640 East Main Street
Ridge Spring, South Carolina
(803) 685-7547

Ridge Spring's two-block downtown doesn't merit a traffic light. But worn wooden walls and floors, retro-cool Formica tables, and a robust menu full of dishes crafted from local farmers make Juniper worth a stop here. Finding this gem in a town with a mere 738 residents is a pleasant surprise rivaled only by those on the menu. Chef Brandon Veilie, who served as a cook for the Marine Corps, mixes Southern staples and creative cooking in dishes such as flash-fried collard greens, whiskey-infused gravy, and peach semifreddo.

Juniper's Peach Gazpacho

This Southern version of the quintessential summer soup is sweet and tangy.

1	Tbsp. black sesame seeds
1	Tbsp. sesame seeds
½	(11-oz.) can mandarin oranges in light syrup
2	cups vegetable juice
2	cups diced peaches
1½	cups diced seedless cucumber
¾	cup diced tomato
½	cup diced red bell pepper
½	cup diced green bell pepper
1	Tbsp. sugar
3	Tbsp. minced red onion
1	Tbsp. red wine vinegar
1	tsp. ground cumin
1	tsp. chopped fresh cilantro
½	tsp. fine sea salt
¼	tsp. freshly ground black pepper
1	garlic clove, minced

1. Heat sesame seeds in a small nonstick skillet over medium heat, stirring often, 2 to 3 minutes or until toasted and fragrant.
2. Drain and chop mandarin oranges, reserving ¼ cup light syrup. Stir together sesame seeds, chopped oranges, light syrup, and remaining ingredients in a large bowl. Cover and chill at least 30 minutes. Serve in small chilled bowls.
Makes 7 cups.

JUNIPER

LUNCH:
MONDAY - SAT
11-2:

CL

THURSDA

RESERV

SUNDAY

11

FOR UPCOMING NE
LLOW US ON F.
85.754
hot

Juniper's South Carolina Peach Semifreddo

This tastes lighter than you might expect for a dessert with so many good things going on.

Crust

20	gingersnaps, finely crushed (about 1¼ cups)
¼	cup unsalted butter, melted

Pecan Praline

½	cup coarsely chopped pecans
½	cup sugar

Semifreddo

1	cup heavy cream
2	Tbsp. powdered sugar
3	cups peeled and finely chopped fresh peaches (4 medium)
½	cup granulated sugar, divided
⅛	tsp. kosher salt
6	egg yolks
½	tsp. vanilla extract

Topping

1½	cups peeled and sliced peaches (2 medium)
1	Tbsp. sugar

1. Prepare Crust: Preheat oven to 350°. Stir together crushed gingersnaps and butter. Press cookie mixture onto bottom of a lightly greased 9-inch springform pan. Bake at 350° for 10 minutes. Cool completely on a wire rack (about 30 minutes).

2. Prepare Pecan Praline: Bake pecans at 350° in a single layer in a shallow pan 8 to 10 minutes or until toasted and fragrant, stirring halfway through. Transfer to a bowl, and lightly grease a baking sheet.

3. Sprinkle sugar in a small heavy saucepan; place over medium heat, and cook, gently shaking pan over heat, 5 to 6 minutes or until sugar melts and turns a light amber brown. Immediately stir in pecans, and cook for 30 seconds. Quickly and carefully pour hot caramelized sugar mixture onto prepared baking sheet. Let praline cool and harden (about 15 minutes). Break into pieces, and finely chop.

4. Prepare Semifreddo: Beat heavy cream until foamy; gradually add powdered sugar, beating until soft peaks form. Stir together chopped peaches, ¼ cup granulated sugar, and salt in a large bowl.

5. Whisk together remaining ¼ cup granulated sugar and egg yolks in top of a double boiler. Bring water just to a simmer in bottom pan, and cook egg yolk mixture, whisking constantly, 4 minutes or until thick and pale and thermometer registers 160°. Remove pan from heat. Fill a large bowl with ice; place top pan of double boiler in ice, and let stand, stirring often, 3 minutes or until chilled. Stir in vanilla.

6. Fold whipped cream and half of Pecan Praline into peach mixture. Pour mixture into prepared crust; place plastic wrap directly onto filling. Freeze 8 to 24 hours. Transfer to refrigerator. Let stand in refrigerator 3 hours to soften slightly.

7. Prepare Topping: Toss sliced peaches with sugar in a medium bowl; let stand 10 minutes or until sugar is dissolved.

8. Gently run a knife around edge of semifreddo to loosen. Remove sides of pan. Cut semifreddo into slices. Spoon Peach Topping over each slice, and sprinkle with remaining Pecan Praline.
Makes 8 to 10 servings.

The Trappe Door

23 West Washington Street
Greenville, South Carolina
(864) 451-7490

If a Belgian restaurant owned by an Australian and located in a basement in Greenville, South Carolina, strikes you as odd, well, just go with it. Thanks to the Trappe Door, "Hey, Honey! Let's go get us some Belgian food tonight!" is fast becoming a common refrain in Greenville. What's not to love about amazing fries, 12 varieties of mayonnaise, artisanal beer, and light-as-a-cloud yeasted waffles? In Belgium, meals are events savored with family and friends, a philosophy that feels right at home in the Deep South. That tradition, along with hardy food, beer, wine, and even absinthe, make the Trappe Door a hideaway you'll want to visit.

The Trappe Door's Carbonnade à la Flamande

Beer and beef star in this traditional Belgian stew.

1   (3-lb.) boneless chuck roast, cut into 1-inch pieces
1   tsp. salt
1   tsp. freshly ground pepper
3   tsp. olive oil, divided
1   onion, sliced
¼   cup sugar
¼   cup all-purpose flour
1   (12-oz.) bottle dark Belgian Abbey beer
2   cups beef broth
3   Tbsp. Dijon mustard
3   sprigs thyme
1   bay leaf
1   Tbsp. red wine vinegar

1. Sprinkle beef with salt and pepper; cook in batches, in 2 tsp. hot oil in a large skillet over medium-high heat, stirring occasionally, 4 minutes or until browned on all sides.

2. Meanwhile, sauté onion in remaining 1 tsp. oil in a large Dutch oven 5 minutes or until nicely browned. Add sugar, and cook, stirring constantly, 30 seconds or until sugar is bubbly and turns golden brown. (Be careful not to burn.) Add beef to Dutch oven, stirring to coat. Sprinkle with flour, stirring until flour is incorporated and beef and onions become sticky and thick. Stir in beer, broth, and mustard. Add thyme sprigs and bay leaf. Cover, reduce heat, and simmer 3 hours or until beef is tender, stirring occasionally. Discard thyme sprigs and bay leaf. Stir in vinegar. **Makes 7½ cups.**

Note: We tested with Brother Thelonious beer.

Trappe Door Moules Marinière

For the Belgian national meal, serve these delicious mussels with Belgian Frites and mayonnaise.

Fish Stock*

1	leek
2	lb. fish bones from a local seafood market
2	Tbsp. black peppercorns
3	celery ribs, coarsely chopped
1	onion, quartered
1	large carrot, coarsely chopped
¼	bunch parsley
6	sprigs thyme
2	bay leaves

Mussels

2	lb. fresh mussels, scrubbed and debearded
3	Tbsp. finely chopped shallots (2 medium)
2	garlic cloves, minced
2	Tbsp. olive oil
½	cup dry white wine
¼	tsp. kosher salt
¼	tsp. freshly ground pepper
1	Tbsp. unsalted butter
1	Tbsp. chopped fresh parsley

1. Prepare Fish Stock: Remove and discard root end of leek. Cut in half lengthwise, and rinse thoroughly under cold running water to remove grit and sand. Cut leek into 1-inch pieces. Bring 4 quarts water, leek, fish bones, and next 7 ingredients to a boil in an 8-quart stockpot. Cover, reduce heat, and simmer 3 hours. Pour through a fine wire-mesh strainer into a large bowl. Discard solids. Set aside ½ cup stock to prepare mussels. Let remaining stock cool, and freeze in zip-top plastic freezer bags up to 6 months.

2. Prepare Mussels: Pick through mussels carefully, making sure all are closed. (If any is open, tap it gently with your finger. If it doesn't close, it is dead and should be discarded.) Sauté shallots and garlic in hot oil in a large stockpot over medium-high heat 1 minute. Add reserved ½ cup fish stock and white wine; cook 30 seconds, stirring to loosen particles from bottom of skillet. Add mussels, salt and pepper. Cover and cook 8 minutes or until shells open. Discard any that do not open. Add butter and parsley, stirring until butter melts. Season with additional salt and pepper, if desired. Divide mussels and stock among 4 bowls. **Makes 4 servings.**

*The mussels dish requires only ½ cup seafood stock, so you'll have about 15 cups more left over (all of which can be frozen for future batches or other uses). As an alternative to making the stock, you can use a dry soup base (such as Penzeys Seafood Soup Base and Seasoning) to prepare ½ cup stock, substitute ½ cup clam juice, or ask your favorite seafood restaurant if they'll sell you ½ cup stock.

Trappe Door Belgian Frites

These terrific Belgian fries, fried twice at different temperatures, are crispy on the outside and fluffy on the inside.

3	baking potatoes (2½ lb.)
	Vegetable oil
	Kosher salt
	Mayonnaise

1. Peel potatoes. Cut into sticks that are ¼ inch thick and about 3 inches long. Place in cold water immediately to keep them from oxidizing, and let them stand in the water for about 30 minutes to help release starch.

2. Drain potatoes, and blot dry with paper towels.

Pour oil to depth of 1 inch into a 5-qt. Dutch oven; heat to 325°. Fry potatoes, in batches, 5 minutes, stirring once to separate. (Fries will be soft but should not have any color.) Drain on a baking sheet covered with paper towels, let cool to room temperature. (This can be done several hours ahead of time.) Reserve cooking oil.

3. Reheat oil to 375°. Return potatoes to oil, and fry 2 to 3 minutes or until golden brown. Drain on a baking sheet covered with fresh paper towels; season with salt. Serve with mayonnaise. **Makes 4 to 6 servings.**

Trappe Door Belgian Waffles

These yeasted waffles are incredible: crispy on the outside, not too sweet, and so very light. Be sure to use a very large bowl to give the batter room to rise.

1	(¼-oz.) envelope active dry yeast
¼	cup warm water (100° to 110°)
1½	cups warm milk (100° to 110°), divided
2	egg yolks
3	Tbsp. vegetable oil
3	Tbsp. unsalted butter, melted
¼	cup sugar
⅛	tsp. salt
2	cups all-purpose flour
1	tsp. vanilla extract
2	egg whites

Toppings: ice cream, fresh fruit, whipped cream, powdered sugar

1. Combine yeast and warm water (100° to 110°) in a 1-cup glass measuring cup; let stand 5 minutes. Whisk together ¾ cup warm milk and egg yolks in a very large bowl. Whisk in oil and butter, followed by yeast mixture, sugar, and salt. Sift flour into yeast mixture in 3 or 4 additions, alternating with remaining ¾ cup milk, and stirring with a wooden spoon after each addition until a smooth batter forms. Stir in vanilla.

2. Beat egg whites at high speed with an electric mixer until soft peaks form. Gently fold egg whites into batter. Cover with a cloth, and let rise in a warm place (85°), free from drafts, 1 hour or until batter is at least doubled in bulk.

3. Cook batter in batches in a preheated, oiled Belgian-style waffle iron until golden. Serve warm, topped with ice cream, fresh fruit, whipped cream, and powdered sugar. **Makes 10 waffles.**

SOUNDTRACK:

"Show Me What I'm Looking For" by Carolina Liar

"Birmingham" by the Charleston band Shovels & Rope

"Don't Think I Don't Think About It" by Darius Rucker

"Charleston" by Louis Prima

"Haywire" by South Carolina native Josh Turner

Best Buns Bread Co.
←

↑
Bayou Bakery Coffee
Bar & Eatery

Something Different
Country Store
and Deli
↙

↖ The Black Sheep

Arlington, Virginia

PORKORN
Salted Caramel Peanut Popcorn with Allan Benton's Bacon

Bayou Bakery Coffee Bar & Eatery

↙ Grady's Barbecue

Dish
↓

↖ The Admiral

North Carolina • Virginia

UP the COAST

Washington, D.C. • Maryland

Papermoon Diner ↙

The Main Ingredient ↓

Cafe Hon ↑

Out of the Fire ↑

Tune Inn ↗

The Crab Claw Restaurant ↙

SERVING HOT PIT COOKED BAR-B-Q PORK
Specializing In Pig Pickings
Gradys Bar-B-Q
3096 Arrington Bridge Rd.
Dudley, NC 28333
Date June 29 2012

The Crab Claw, Inc.
ST. MICHAELS
MARYLAND
745-2900

The Admiral

400 Haywood Road
Asheville, North Carolina
(828) 252-2541

Among the hipsters in up-and-coming West Asheville, you'll find my favorite restaurant in town. The plain, cinder-block building sports a mid-century modern feel, and greatness lurks within. The Admiral shows its Southern pride with miniature Mason jars of pimiento cheese and its cool take on Southern classics. Accordingly, you're likely to find it jammed with locals who come for dishes such as barbecued quail, pepper-spiked creamed corn, and refined specialty drinks like the Dark and Stormy, concocted with house-made ginger ale that's spicy enough to make you stand up and salute. Chef Elliott Moss's cuisine impresses and delights—and you get the added fun of watching it come to life in the restaurant's open kitchen.

The Admiral's Charred Poblano Creamed Corn

This herbaceous corn has a peppery kick.

1	poblano pepper
1	jalapeño pepper
½	cup coarsely chopped onion
3	garlic cloves, minced
1½	tsp. vegetable oil
1	cup heavy cream
1	tsp. salt
¾	tsp. freshly ground pepper
1	cup loosely packed fresh cilantro leaves
¼	cup loosely packed fresh basil leaves
4	cups fresh corn kernels (10 ears)
2	Tbsp. fresh lime juice
¼	cup sour cream

Garnish: fresh basil leaves

1. Broil poblano and jalapeño peppers on an aluminum foil-lined baking sheet 5 inches from heat 3 to 4 minutes on each side or until peppers look blistered. Place peppers in a zip-top plastic freezer bag; seal and let stand 10 minutes to loosen skins. Peel peppers; remove and discard seeds. Coarsely chop peppers.
2. Sauté onion and garlic in hot oil in a large skillet over medium-high heat 4 minutes or until tender. Stir in chopped roasted peppers, cream, salt, and pepper; bring to a simmer. Remove from heat; let cool 15 minutes.
3. Process cream mixture, cilantro, and basil in a blender until smooth. Return cream mixture to skillet. Stir in corn kernels and lime juice; bring to a boil over medium-high heat. Reduce heat, and simmer 4 minutes or until corn is tender. Remove from heat; stir in sour cream. Serve immediately. **Makes 4 to 6 servings.**

The Admiral's Peach Brûlée

Fresh peaches make the basic brûlée (crisp top, cool creamy center) even more satisfying

2   cups coarsely chopped unpeeled fresh peaches
¾   cup sugar, divided
1   (3-inch) piece vanilla bean, split lengthwise
2   cups heavy cream
5   egg yolks
8   tsp. sugar
⅛   tsp. fine sea salt

1. Preheat oven to 350°. Combine peaches and ¼ cup sugar in a small saucepan; cook, stirring often, over medium heat 20 minutes or until peaches are soft and mixture is thickened. Process peach mixture in a food processor until smooth, stopping to scrape down sides.

2. Scrape seeds from vanilla bean; add seeds and bean to cream in a small saucepan. Bring to a simmer over low heat, and cook, stirring often, 6 minutes. Discard vanilla bean.

3. Whisk remaining ½ cup sugar and egg yolks in a medium bowl 3 minutes or until thick and pale. Gradually stir about one-fourth of hot cream mixture into yolks; add yolk mixture to remaining hot cream mixture, stirring constantly. Stir in peach purée.

4. Pour mixture evenly into 8 (4-oz.) shallow crème brûlée ramekins. Place ramekins in a large shallow pan. Add hot tap water (about 115°) to depth of ½ inch in pan (or halfway up sides of ramekins). Cover loosely with a large piece of aluminum foil.

5. Bake at 350° for 20 minutes or until custards are set (they should jiggle like set gelatin when the ramekins are bumped). Remove ramekins from water bath; place on a wire rack. Cool completely (about 1 hour). Cover and chill at least 3 hours.

6. Sprinkle each serving with 1 tsp. sugar. Brown with a kitchen torch, sweeping it over the surface until the sugar is browned and caramelized but not burned. Immediately sprinkle a pinch of sea salt into the hot sugar. **Makes 8 servings.**

Note: We tested with shallow ramekins that measure 3½ inches wide and 1¾ inches deep.

Dish

1220 Thomas Avenue
Charlotte, North Carolina
(704) 344-0343

Sunshine and happiness soak my favorite lunch spot in the Queen City. Sitting down in Penny Craver and Maggie Stubbs's restaurant is like pulling up a chair in my grandmother's breakfast room. Vintage plates line the walls. Waitresses wear vintage aprons. Vinyl booths and bar stools seem pulled straight from an Arlo Guthrie song. And oh, the comfort food. It's pork chops, chicken livers, and meatloaf—and pies and cookies too. No doubt you'll leave stuffed and a little sunnier for the experience.

Dish's Chicken & Dumplings

Hearty and rich—these may be the best dumplings ever. To save time, you can buy a whole deli-roasted chicken instead of roasting your own.

Chicken

1   (3½-lb.) whole chicken
1   Tbsp. vegetable oil
¼   tsp. kosher salt
⅛   tsp. freshly ground pepper

Dumplings

3   large eggs
10 Tbsp. butter, melted
1   tsp. kosher salt
2⅔ cups all-purpose flour
Parchment paper

Stock

¾   cup chopped onion
2   Tbsp. onion powder
1   Tbsp. celery salt
1   Tbsp. coarsely ground pepper
½   tsp. garlic powder

Roux

10 Tbsp. butter
10 Tbsp. all-purpose flour

Garnish

Flat-leaf parsley leaves

1. Prepare Chicken: Preheat oven to 350°. If chicken has giblets, remove them, and reserve for another use. Rinse chicken, and pat dry. Place chicken in a 13- x 9-inch baking dish, breast side up; brush entire bird with oil, and sprinkle with salt and pepper. Bake at 350° for 1 hour and 10 minutes or until a meat thermometer inserted into thickest portion of thigh registers 165°. Cool 30 minutes. Remove chicken skin and bones, and reserve them for stock. Shred meat with two forks, or coarsely chop. Set aside.

2. Prepare Dumplings: Whisk eggs in a large bowl. Add melted butter and salt, whisking until smooth. Gradually add flour, stirring until mixture forms a ball. Turn dough out onto a lightly floured surface, and roll into a 12-inch square on a lightly floured surface. (Dough should be about ¼ inch thick.) Let dough rest, uncovered, 10 minutes. Cut dough into 2-inch squares. Place dumplings on a large parchment paper-lined baking sheet. Cover and chill until ready to cook.

3. Prepare Stock: Bring 8 cups water and reserved chicken skin and bones to a boil in a 6-qt. Dutch oven. Remove from heat; strain stock into a large bowl. Discard skin and bones. Return stock to Dutch oven. Add onion and next 4 ingredients; bring to a boil. Add dumplings to boiling stock. Reduce heat to medium; cover and cook for 30 minutes, stirring often.

4. Prepare Roux: Melt butter in a 2-qt. saucepan over medium heat. Whisk in flour until smooth. Cook 10 minutes or until light brown, stirring constantly.

5. Stir roux and shredded chicken into stock; reduce heat to medium-low, and cook, uncovered, 20 minutes or until thickened, stirring often. Season with additional celery salt, if desired. **Makes 10½ cups.**

Dish's Vanilla-Bourbon Sweet Potato Pie

Neither too sweet nor too boozy, this pie is still definitely an indulgence.

Filling

3	large sweet potatoes (2¼ lb.)
1	tsp. salt
¾	cup granulated sugar
2	Tbsp. vanilla extract
1	Tbsp. bourbon or whiskey
2	large eggs
¼	cup all-purpose flour

Crust

3	cups graham cracker crumbs (about 20¼ sheets)
½	cup granulated sugar
½	cup butter, melted

Topping

½	cup firmly packed light brown sugar
1	cup pecan halves
3	Tbsp. honey
1½	Tbsp. bourbon or whiskey

1. Prepare Filling: Bring sweet potatoes, salt, and water to cover to a boil in a large Dutch oven over high heat; cook 35 minutes or until tender. Drain. Peel potatoes, and mash with a potato masher in a large bowl. Let cool slightly.

OVERHEARD: "It's so dark out you have to light a second match to see if the first one caught."

Now that's dark. I was driving in the Great Smoky Mountains near Asheville one night last summer and pulled over in a field to watch the most amazing lightning bug show. It was a sight you would find only far away from the light pollution of a city.

Whisk together sugar, vanilla, bourbon, and eggs in a medium bowl. Stir sugar mixture into sweet potatoes. Stir in flour.

2. Prepare Crust: Preheat oven to 350°. Stir together graham cracker crumbs, sugar, and melted butter; press mixture on bottom and up sides of a 9-inch springform pan. Bake at 350° for 10 minutes. Pour sweet potato mixture into prepared crust. Bake at 350° for 55 to 60 minutes or until center is set.

3. Prepare Topping: Remove pie from oven, and sprinkle top of hot pie with brown sugar; arrange pecan halves decoratively around edge of pie. Stir together honey and bourbon in a small bowl; drizzle over top of pie. Cool in pan on a wire rack 2 hours. Gently run a sharp knife around edge of pie to loosen; remove sides of pan. Place pie on a serving platter; cover and chill 24 hours. Serve chilled. **Makes 10 to 12 servings.**

Note: If you have an older springform pan that does not seal tightly, wrap the outside of the pan in foil before making the pie to prevent leaking.

Dish

Meatloaf and chicken and dumplings sound good but not cutting edge. Gingham and grandma's old china don't exude hip. And yet? Despite being decorated straight out of *Ladies Home Journal* circa 1957, Dish oozes cool. I mean, the waitresses wear headbands in that stylish, Free People catalog way, without looking like Aunt Jemima or an Occupy protestor. Often when I go to übercool places, I'm overcome with the desire to do something NOT cool, like wear a tie or say, "Hey, skinny model chick, watch this!" and break out into a full-on Watusi. However, I am totally comfy at the (very cool) Dish. My guess? It's the comfort food, done to perfection.

North Carolina

Grady's Barbecue

3096 Arrington Bridge Road
Dudley, North Carolina
(919) 735-7243

The woodpile outside this little white building—a mix of ash, hickory, and oak—is testament to the care Grady's applies to its 'cue. But ask Steve Grady to name the ingredients in his vinegar-based barbecue sauce, and the old-timer just raises an eyebrow. So, sorry folks, I can't reveal that recipe here. Still, there are some other secrets that keep a wide cross section of North Carolinians (the parking lot sports both battered pickup trucks and new Mercedes convertibles) coming to this isolated spot. Gerrie Grady, who is all smiles and hugs, slipped me two of those famous recipes: her sweet lemonade and perfect black-eyed peas. (Shhh, don't tell Steve.)

Grady's Sweet Lemonade

Make sure to ask for the real stuff when you order this Southern classic. (Grady's also offers a powdered-mix version.) When making it at home, start with 1½ cups of the sugar, and add more to suit your taste.

8   large lemons
2   qt. cold water
1½ to 2 cups sugar

1. Cut lemons in half; squeeze juice into a measuring cup to equal 1 cup, using a reamer to get out as much pulp as possible from the fruit. Add the juice, pulp, and, yes, even the seeds to a 1-gal. pitcher (or a big, clean pickle jar) with the cold water. Add sugar, and stir vigorously until it dissolves. (No need to heat it; just stir, and have faith.) Serve over ice. **Makes 10 cups.**

Grady's Black-eyed Peas

The secret here is the peanut oil, which lends richness to these tasty peas.

4   cups fresh black-eyed peas (about 1⅓ lb.)
¼   cup peanut oil
2   tsp. salt
⅛   tsp. sugar
⅛   tsp. freshly ground pepper
Liquid from hot peppers in vinegar
½   cup chopped white onion

1. Place peas in a 4-qt. saucepan; add enough water to cover peas by 1 inch. Stir in oil, salt, sugar, and pepper. Bring to a boil over high heat; partially cover, reduce heat, and simmer 1 hour or until tender. Keep a watchful eye on the pot, and add cold water if necessary to keep water level above the peas. Serve with a slotted spoon. Season with liquid from hot peppers in vinegar, and top with onion. **Makes 8 servings.**

Bayou Bakery Coffee Bar & Eatery

1515 North Courthouse Road
Arlington, Virginia
(703) 243-2410

Our nation's capital was situated in a swamp. Never let it be said that ol' George Washington didn't have a sense of humor—or a taste for irony. In any event, what to do when you're in a swamp? Chow down on some bayou classics, of course. And there's no better place to do that near the district than at Bayou Bakery, which is owned by one of my favorite chefs: David Guas. The restaurant itself is a bright and airy place, with fun nods back to David's native Louisiana. Happily, it's where he serves up many of his most famous dishes. Trust me, once you taste this bacon-studded blue cheese dip, you'll wonder why you haven't made it for every football game and backyard barbecue.

Bayou Bakery's Bacon and Blue Cheese Dip

This creamy dip slaps you with fresh chives and the funk of good blue cheese.

2   cups crumbled blue cheese
1½   cups mayonnaise
1½   cups sour cream
¾   cup cooked and crumbled bacon (about 8 slices)
1½   tsp. freshly ground pepper
1   tsp. hot sauce
Salt to taste
2   tsp. chopped fresh chives
Kettle-cooked potato chips

1. Stir together first 6 ingredients in a medium bowl. Cover and chill 2 to 8 hours. Stir in salt to taste. Sprinkle with chives. Serve with potato chips. **Makes 12 servings.**

Bayou Bakery's Gulf Shrimp Roll

This is just like a fine po'boy, just in a denser roll.

1	tsp. salt
1½	lb. peeled, medium-size raw Gulf shrimp
½	cup mayonnaise
¼	cup chopped green onions
1	Tbsp. Creole mustard
2	Tbsp. diced red onion
½	tsp. celery seed
¼	tsp. salt
⅛	tsp. freshly ground pepper
6	oblong potato rolls or pretzel rolls
2	Tbsp. sliced green onions

1. Pour water to depth of 3 inches in a large saucepan; stir in salt. Bring to a boil; add shrimp. Remove from heat; let stand 2 minutes or just until shrimp turn pink. Drain and plunge into ice water to stop the cooking process; drain. Chop shrimp.

2. Stir together mayonnaise and next 6 ingredients in a medium bowl. Gently fold in shrimp. Spoon salad into rolls; sprinkle with sliced green onions. **Makes 6 servings.**

{ PUNCH DAT CARD }
A BAKER'S DOZEN
...ive one punch per purchase of a
...or tea beverage at Bayou
...Bar & Eatery. After 12
...one is on us!
...cash value.
...beverages.

{ PUNCH DAT CARD }
A BAKER'S DOZEN
Receive one punch per purchase of a
coffee or tea beverage at Bayou
Bakery Coffee Bar & Eatery. After 12
...unches, your next one is on us!

Management reserves all rights. No cash value.
Valid only on coffee and tea beverages.

7 8 9 10 11 12 13

Bayou Bakery's Old-Fashioned Chocolate Pudding

Rich and chocolaty, this recipe whups the instant puddings of the world.

½	cup sugar
3	Tbsp. cornstarch
2	Tbsp. unsweetened cocoa
¼	tsp. salt
5	egg yolks
2	cups milk
1	tsp. vanilla extract
4	oz. semisweet or bittersweet chocolate (preferably 58%-62% cacao), finely chopped
2	Tbsp. unsalted butter

Garnishes: whipped cream, grated chocolate

1. Whisk together first 5 ingredients in a medium bowl. Bring milk to a boil in a medium saucepan over medium-high heat, stirring often. Gradually whisk one-fourth hot milk into egg yolk mixture. Add remaining milk, whisking constantly.

2. Pour mixture into a clean medium saucepan (necessary to prevent the pudding from scorching). Cook over medium-low heat, whisking constantly, until the pudding is glossy and thick and reaches a temperature of at least 160° (about 4 minutes). Remove from heat; stir in vanilla.

3. Transfer pudding to a medium bowl. Add finely chopped chocolate and butter, whisking until chocolate and butter melt. Serve warm, or spoon into 6 (4-oz.) custard cups or ramekins. Place plastic wrap directly onto warm custard (to prevent a film from forming), and chill 4 hours or up to 3 days. **Makes 6 servings.**

Bayou Bakery's Dat-O's

Imagine a fresh Oreo the size of your head. That's a Dat-O. The bakery also sells Dis-O's, so you can press your nose to the bakery glass and ask for Dis one or Dat one.

Cookies

3	cups all-purpose flour
1⅓	cups unsweetened cocoa
1	tsp. kosher salt
¾	tsp. baking soda
¾	tsp. baking powder
1¼	cups unsalted butter, softened
3¼	cups granulated sugar
2	large eggs

Parchment paper

Cream Filling

½	cup unsalted butter
½	cup shortening
1	(4-inch) piece vanilla bean, split lengthwise
2	tsp. vanilla extract
4¾	cups powdered sugar, sifted

1. Prepare Cookies: Preheat oven to 375°. Sift together flour and cocoa into a large bowl. Whisk in salt, baking soda, and baking powder.

2. Beat butter and sugar at medium speed with a heavy-duty electric stand mixer about 5 minutes or until creamy, using paddle attachment. Add eggs, 1 at a time, beating just until yellow disappears. Add flour mixture, and beat on low just until combined. Drop mixture by ⅓ cupfuls onto parchment paper-lined baking sheets. Bake at 375° for 16 to 17 minutes or until barely set and crackled on top. (Cookies will continue to firm up as they cool.) Cool on pans 2 minutes; transfer to a wire rack, and cool completely (about 30 minutes).

3. Prepare Cream Filling: Beat butter and shortening at medium speed with a heavy-duty electric stand mixer about 2 minutes or until creamy, using paddle attachment. Scrape seeds from vanilla bean, and add seeds to butter mixture; discard bean piece. Add vanilla to butter mixture; beat at medium speed 1 minute. Add powdered sugar in three additions, beating until blended after each addition.

4. Spread filling on flat side of half the cookies (about ⅓ cup per cookie); top with remaining cookies, flat side down, pressing down gently until filling comes to cookie edges. **Makes 8 sandwich cookies.**

Best Buns Bread Co.

4010 Campbell Avenue
Arlington, Virginia
(703) 578-1500

This sunny bakery puts the average chain coffee house to shame—shame, I say. Walk in, and the smell of freshly baked goodness covers you like a warm comforter. Happy bakers in white coats scurry about, filling orders, and whisking one amazing pan out of the oven after another. It's enough to break even the most ardent Atkins follower. When I'm in town, I go for an early breakfast, hauling along my favorite newspaper and ordering an oven-baked treat and a giant cup of coffee. What a way to start the day.

Best Buns
Bacon-Cheddar Scones

Here's an entire country-boy breakfast in one delicious, slightly salty scone.

1	cup sugar, divided
2	cups all-purpose flour
2	cups cake flour
1½	Tbsp. baking powder
1	tsp. sea salt
1	cup cold lard, cut up
1½	cups (6 oz.) shredded sharp Cheddar cheese
6	cooked bacon slices, crumbled
1	cup milk
2	large eggs
Parchment paper	
½	cup maple syrup

1. Preheat oven to 450°. Stir together ½ cup sugar, all-purpose flour, and next 3 ingredients in a large bowl. Cut lard into flour mixture with pastry blender or fork until crumbly. Add cheese and bacon, and toss to combine. Whisk together milk and eggs in a medium bowl; add to the flour mixture, stirring just until dry ingredients are moistened and a dough forms.
2. Drop dough by ¼ cupfuls onto parchment paper-lined baking sheets. Whisk together remaining ½ cup sugar and maple syrup. Brush tops of dough with syrup mixture.
3. Bake at 450° for 10 to 12 minutes or until lightly browned. **Makes 1½ dozen.**

Best Buns
Blueberry-Lemon Muffins

This is the best blueberry muffin—sweet and tart, with a crunchy streusel topping.

Streusel

½	cup powdered sugar
6	Tbsp. all-purpose flour
¼	cup unsalted cold butter, cut up

Muffins

2	cups cake flour
1¼	cups all-purpose flour
1	cup granulated sugar
5	tsp. baking powder
½	tsp. fine sea salt
3	large eggs
¾	cup whole milk
¾	cup unsalted butter, melted
1	tsp. lemon zest
1	tsp. lemon extract
1⅓	cups frozen blueberries

Jumbo paper baking cups
Vegetable cooking spray

Syrup

¾	cup granulated sugar
⅔	cup fresh lemon juice

1. Prepare Streusel: Stir together sugar and flour in a medium bowl. Cut butter into mixture with a pastry blender or fork until crumbly. Cover and chill.

2. Prepare Muffins: Preheat oven to 350°. Whisk together first 5 ingredients in a large bowl; make a well in center of mixture. Whisk eggs in another large bowl. Whisk in milk and next 3 ingredients; add to dry mixture, stirring just until moistened. Fold in blueberries.

3. Place baking cups in 2 (6-cup) Texas muffin pans. Coat cups with cooking spray. Spoon batter into cups, filling two-thirds full. Sprinkle with streusel. Bake at 350° for 30 minutes or until golden.

4. Prepare Syrup: While muffins bake, combine sugar and lemon juice in a small bowl, whisking until sugar dissolves.

5. Drizzle syrup over hot muffins. Cool in pans on a wire rack 3 minutes. Remove muffins from pans to wire racks, and cool completely (about 30 minutes). **Makes 1 dozen.**

Shirlington • (703) 578-1500

Best Buns
English Toffee Cookies

Chewy, sticky, and rich, these are a chocolate-and-caramel lover's heaven.

1	cup all-purpose flour
¼	tsp. coarse sea salt
½	tsp. baking soda
7	Tbsp. butter, softened
⅓	cup firmly packed light brown sugar
¼	cup granulated sugar
1	large egg
¼	tsp. vanilla extract
4	(1.4-oz.) chocolate-covered toffee candy bars, chopped (1¼ cups)
½	cup semisweet chocolate morsels

Parchment paper

1. Preheat oven to 350°. Whisk together first 3 ingredients in a medium bowl. In a large bowl, beat butter, brown sugar, and granulated sugar at medium speed with an electric mixer until creamy (about 1 minute); add egg and vanilla, beating just until yellow disappears. Add flour mixture; beat at low speed until combined, scraping sides of bowl once. Stir in chopped candy bars and chocolate morsels.

2. Drop dough by rounded tablespoonfuls 3 inches apart onto parchment paper-lined baking sheets. Bake at 350° for 13 minutes or until crispy around the edges and soft in the middle. Cool on baking sheets 2 minutes. Transfer to wire racks, and cool completely (about 20 minutes). **Makes 20 cookies.**

Note: A small (1½-inch-diameter) scoop holds a rounded tablespoon and quickly portions the dough for these cookies.

Best Buns Ginger Crinkle Cookies

These ginormous (5-inch!) gingersnaps are laced with spice and have a hint of orange that becomes more pronounced if you chill the dough before baking, making them ideal make-ahead treats.

1⅓	cups bread flour
1¼	cups all-purpose flour
2¼	tsp. baking soda
2¼	tsp. ground ginger
1¼	tsp. ground cinnamon
½	tsp. ground cloves
¼	tsp. fine sea salt
1¼	cups firmly packed brown sugar
1	extra-large egg
¾	cup plus 2 Tbsp. canola oil
⅓	cup dark molasses
⅓	cup minced candied orange peel
⅓	cup minced crystallized ginger

Granulated sugar

1. Whisk together first 7 ingredients in a medium bowl. Combine brown sugar and egg in a bowl of a heavy-duty electric stand mixer; beat at medium speed until well blended. Gradually add oil, followed by molasses, beating until combined. Reduce speed to low; add flour mixture all at once, and beat until smooth. Stir in candied orange peel and ginger. Cover and chill 3 to 6 hours to let the flavors settle in, if desired.

2. Preheat oven to 350°. Drop ¼-cup portion of dough into a small bowl of granulated sugar. Roll to coat. Shape into a ball. Roll ball in sugar once more. Repeat with remaining dough.

3. Place balls 2 inches apart on ungreased baking sheets. Flatten slightly with bottom of a glass dipped in sugar. Bake at 350° for 14 to 16 minutes or until cookies are crinkled and lightly browned. Cool on baking sheets 5 minutes. Transfer to wire racks. **Makes 1 dozen.**

The Black Sheep

901 West Marshall Street
Richmond, Virginia
(804) 648-1300

In a narrow brick building in the Sheep Hill section of town, I found one of my favorite sandwich shops ever. This spot transforms whimsical objects and art into urban chic. And sandwiches served here stretch so long that owner Kevin Roberts names them after famous battleships. Each comes served on a bamboo cutting board with a knife for sectioning. The CSS Virginia—a delectable combination of chicken livers, crusty French bread, and green apples—easily feeds four people. But the Black Sheep is more than just sandwiches. You'll enjoy its fudge-laced peanut butter pie, witty desserts such as the La Brea Tarpit (animal crackers stuck in a chocolate crème brûlée), and my new favorite breakfast, a rich combination of smoked trout, egg, and bacon.

The Black Sheep South Anna Scramble

This decadent fish breakfast has a delicate smoky flavor. The restaurant uses tomato "petals" made by slow-cooking seeded and skinned tomatoes in olive oil with thyme. We substituted softened sun-dried tomatoes.

8	sun-dried tomatoes
3	pasteurized egg yolks
1	Tbsp. fresh lemon juice
1	Tbsp. refrigerated horseradish
¼	tsp. kosher salt
¾	cup butter
2	Tbsp. chopped fresh chives
4	bacon slices
2	cups sliced fresh shiitake mushrooms
1	tsp. butter
6	oz. smoked trout, flaked into ½-inch pieces
6	extra-large eggs, lightly beaten
¼	tsp. freshly ground pepper
8	white bread slices, toasted and halved diagonally

Garnish: chopped fresh chives

1. Bring 1 cup water to a boil in a small saucepan. Remove from heat; add sun-dried tomatoes. Cover and let stand 15 minutes. Drain and thinly slice tomatoes.

2. Process 2 Tbsp. water, egg yolks, and next 3 ingredients in a blender until smooth.

3. Melt ¾ cup butter in a small saucepan over medium-high heat. (Do not brown.) Turn blender on high (with blender lid on and center cap open); immediately add hot butter in a slow, steady stream, pouring through cap opening. Process until thickened. Pour into a small bowl; stir in chives. Cover and keep warm.

4. Cook bacon in a large nonstick skillet over medium heat 6 minutes or until crisp; remove

bacon, and drain on paper towel, reserving 2 Tbsp. drippings in skillet. Crumble bacon.

5. Sauté mushrooms in drippings over medium-high heat 3 minutes or until lightly browned. Add 1 tsp. butter, crumbled bacon, sun-dried tomatoes, and smoked trout. Whisk together eggs and pepper; pour into skillet, and cook, without stirring, 1 minute or until eggs begin to set on bottom. Gently draw cooked edges away from sides of skillet to form large pieces. Cook, stirring occasionally, 2 to 3 minutes or until eggs are thickened and moist. (Do not over stir.)

6. Spoon eggs over toast; drizzle with warm sauce. **Makes 4 servings.**

The Black Sheep Peanut Butter Pie

This is the best peanut butter pie. Its excellent crust and rich fudge layer anchor the tall, thick, and incredibly creamy filling.

Graham Cracker Crust

1¼	cups graham cracker crumbs (about 9 sheets)
7	Tbsp. butter, melted
¼	cup granulated sugar

Fudge Layer

1	cup granulated sugar
⅓	cup evaporated milk
1	Tbsp. light corn syrup
2	oz. bittersweet chocolate, finely chopped
2	Tbsp. creamy peanut butter

Filling

1	envelope unflavored gelatin
⅔	cup cold milk, divided
12	oz. cream cheese, softened
1	cup creamy peanut butter
1⅓	cups powdered sugar
1½	tsp. vanilla extract
1	(16-oz.) container frozen whipped topping, thawed
1	cup finely chopped peanuts

1. Prepare Crust: Preheat oven to 375°. Stir together graham cracker crumbs, butter, and sugar; press mixture evenly onto bottom and

OVERHEARD: "Over yonder."
Southerners and Shakespearian actors are about the only people who say "yonder" any longer. What light through yonder window breaks indeed! I was tracing my family's roots in the James River area and was told to visit a library "over yonder," which is just a tad farther than "down the road a piece."

½ inch up sides of a lightly greased 9-inch springform pan. Bake at 375° for 7 minutes. Cool on a wire rack.

2. Prepare Fudge Layer: Stir together sugar and next 3 ingredients in a medium-size heavy saucepan over medium-high heat, and cook, stirring occasionally, until a candy thermometer registers 234° to 240° (soft ball stage, about 10 minutes). Remove from heat; stir in peanut butter. Pour immediately into prepared crust, and quickly tilt in all directions so that fudge covers bottom of crust. Place in freezer.

3. Prepare Filling: Sprinkle gelatin over ⅓ cup cold milk in a small microwave-safe bowl; let stand 1 minute. Microwave at HIGH 20 seconds or until gelatin dissolves, stirring after 10 seconds. Beat cream cheese and peanut butter at medium-high speed with a heavy-duty electric stand mixer until creamy; gradually add powdered sugar, beating well. Add gelatin mixture, remaining ⅓ cup milk, and vanilla, beating at high speed until creamy. Fold in whipped topping in 3 additions.

4. Pour into prepared crust, and smooth top with back of a spoon (pan will be full). Sprinkle top with peanuts. Cover with plastic wrap, and freeze until firm (about 2 to 4 hours).

5. Remove from freezer; let stand 30 minutes. Remove sides of pan; let stand 30 more minutes. Cut pie into wedges with a warm knife dipped in hot water and wiped dry. (Fudge layer will be quite hard.) Thaw servings in refrigerator until softened (about 2 hours). **Makes 12 servings.**

The Black Sheep

I'm a dude. So any restaurant that sports pop art of Farrah Fawcett (sigh) and gives me a big, honking knife (weaponry!) with my sandwich—a sandwich named for a battleship, no less—well, blam! Fire at will! Instant favorite. Another thing I love about The Black Sheep is that the whole family is in on the job. Son had a dream. Sister tied on an apron. Mama keeps the books. Now that's love—and a great family—which makes for an unforgettable restaurant.

Virginia

Something Different Country Store and Deli

3617 Old Virginia Street
Urbanna, Virginia
(804) 758-8000

An old country store plunked in the middle of a soybean field might not strike casual observers as a hotbed for inventive cooking. But look beyond the ancient butcher-block tables and smoldering barbecue pit. Proprietor Dan Gill is a man of many surprises. With his Tidewater drawl, Dan will regale you about how MSG was developed from kelp or tempt you to try his amazing chile-laced ice cream. His favorite hoecakes are best eaten with a little drizzled molasses—and, he'll point out, they are gluten-free. Dan and his wife, Barbara, also serve a buttermilk pie, the only one I've ever seen that doesn't separate. So drop in, order some iced tea in a Mason jar, and be prepared to sit a spell and hear some fascinating food tales.

Something Different Jalapeño Hoecakes

These are crispy and light, and they give you just the right amount of spicy burn.

2 cups finely ground plain yellow cornmeal
¾ tsp. fine sea salt
¾ tsp. baking soda
¾ tsp. adobo seasoning
¼ cup fresh corn kernels
1 Tbsp. olive oil
¼ small onion
1 jalapeño pepper, stem removed
2 large eggs, lightly beaten
⅔ cup buttermilk
Molasses

1. Whisk together first 4 ingredients in a large bowl. Process corn kernels and next 3 ingredients in a food processor until evenly minced, stopping to scrape down sides. Transfer vegetable mixture to a small bowl, and stir in eggs and buttermilk. Pour buttermilk mixture into cornmeal mixture, and stir just until moistened.

2. Working in batches, pour batter by the tablespoonful onto a hot, lightly greased griddle or large nonstick skillet. Cook hoecakes 1 to 2 minutes or until tops are covered with bubbles and edges look dry; turn and cook 1 minute more. Serve hot with a drizzle of molasses. **Makes 6 to 8 servings.**

Tune Inn

331½ Pennsylvania Avenue Southeast
Washington, DC
(202) 543-2725

*When I think of backroom political deals,
cut with congressmen and senators in
obscure bars just a constituent's throw
from the Capitol, I picture the Tune Inn.
With a logo that looks like a Hells Angels
tattoo, animal heads lining the walls, and
a full bar, the Tune Inn will take the edge
off that appropriations meeting you were
stuck in all day. But behind its rough-
and-tumble appearance, you'll find some
old-school menu treasures well worth
sampling. And, if you happen to spot your
congressmen while there, tell 'em to get
back to work.*

Tune Inn's Corned Beef Hash

This is an amazing hash: not too mushy, not too salty, just right. Cooking the corned beef and potatoes a day ahead reduces the prep time required on serving day. Sauté the hash in single-serving batches for the best browning. At the Tune Inn, eggs cooked over-easy or scrambled are diner favorites.

1   (4-lb.) package corned beef brisket
    with spice packet
2   lb. baking potatoes
2   tsp. salt, divided
1   cup chopped onion
1   cup chopped green bell pepper
1   tsp. freshly ground pepper
3   Tbsp. butter
6   large eggs, prepared any style
Salt and pepper to taste (optional)

1. Place corned beef with spices, fat side up, in a large Dutch oven; cover with water, and bring to a boil over high heat. Cover, reduce heat, and simmer 3 hours or until tender. Remove from heat; uncover and cool at room temperature 1 hour. Cover and chill corned beef in cooking liquid 24 hours.

2. Meanwhile, bring potatoes, 1 tsp. salt, and water to cover to a boil in a Dutch oven over medium-high heat, and cook 25 minutes or until tender. Drain; let cool. Cover and chill 24 hours.

3. Drain corned beef; discard cooking liquid. Trim and discard fat; dice corned beef. Peel potatoes; dice. Toss together corned beef, potatoes, onion, bell pepper, remaining 1 tsp. salt, and pepper in a large bowl.

4. Melt ½ Tbsp. butter in a 12-inch cast-iron skillet over medium-high heat. Add one-sixth of hash (about 1⅓ cups), and cook 3 to 4 minutes or until browned, stirring occasionally. Spoon onto an individual plate; top with 1 egg. Season with salt and pepper, if desired. Repeat procedure with remaining butter, hash, and eggs. **Makes 6 servings.**

Tune Inn's Blackened Salmon Salad

This main-dish salad is as hearty as it is colorful.

Croutons

5	cups (1-inch) French baguette cubes
2	Tbsp. olive oil
2	Tbsp. freshly grated Parmesan cheese
2	Tbsp. dried oregano
½	tsp. salt
½	tsp. freshly ground pepper
2	large garlic cloves, minced (I Tbsp.)

Dressing

½	cup mayonnaise
⅓	cup Dijon mustard
3	Tbsp. sugar
2	Tbsp. white vinegar
2	Tbsp. olive oil
I	tsp. minced fresh oregano
I	tsp. minced fresh basil
I	tsp. minced fresh dill

Salad

⅓	cup walnuts
4	(I½-inch-thick) salmon fillets (about 1¾ lb.)
2	tsp. blackened seasoning
I	Tbsp. olive oil
8	cups torn romaine lettuce
½	cup sweetened dried cranberries

1. Prepare Croutons: Preheat oven to 350°. Place bread cubes in a large bowl; drizzle with 2 Tbsp. oil, tossing to coat. Transfer bread cubes to a lightly greased large baking sheet. Bake at 350° for 8 minutes.

2. Meanwhile, combine cheese and next 4 ingredients in same bowl. Remove bread cubes from oven. Add bread cubes to cheese mixture; toss to coat. Return bread cubes to baking sheet. Bake 8 more minutes or until toasted. Cool completely.

3. Prepare Dressing: Stir together all ingredients in a bowl. Cover and chill.

4. Prepare Salad: Preheat oven to 350°. Bake walnuts in a single layer in a shallow pan at 350° for 5 to 6 minutes or until toasted and fragrant, stirring halfway through.

5. Meanwhile, rub fillets with blackened seasoning. Heat a large skillet over medium-high heat. Add olive oil to pan; add salmon, skin side up. Cook 5 minutes on each side or until desired degree of doneness. Carefully insert a spatula between skin and flesh of salmon. Remove fillets from pan, leaving skin in pan.

6. Combine lettuce and dressing in a large bowl, tossing to coat. Place 2 cups salad mixture on each of 4 plates. Top each with a fillet. Sprinkle salads with walnuts and cranberries. **Makes 4 servings.**

OVERHEARD: "The best thing about this group of candidates is that only one of them can win."

Will Rogers said it, and it still rings true. Washington, D.C., despite its beauty, remains the subject of much ridicule. Politics invites laughter. That, or you cry.

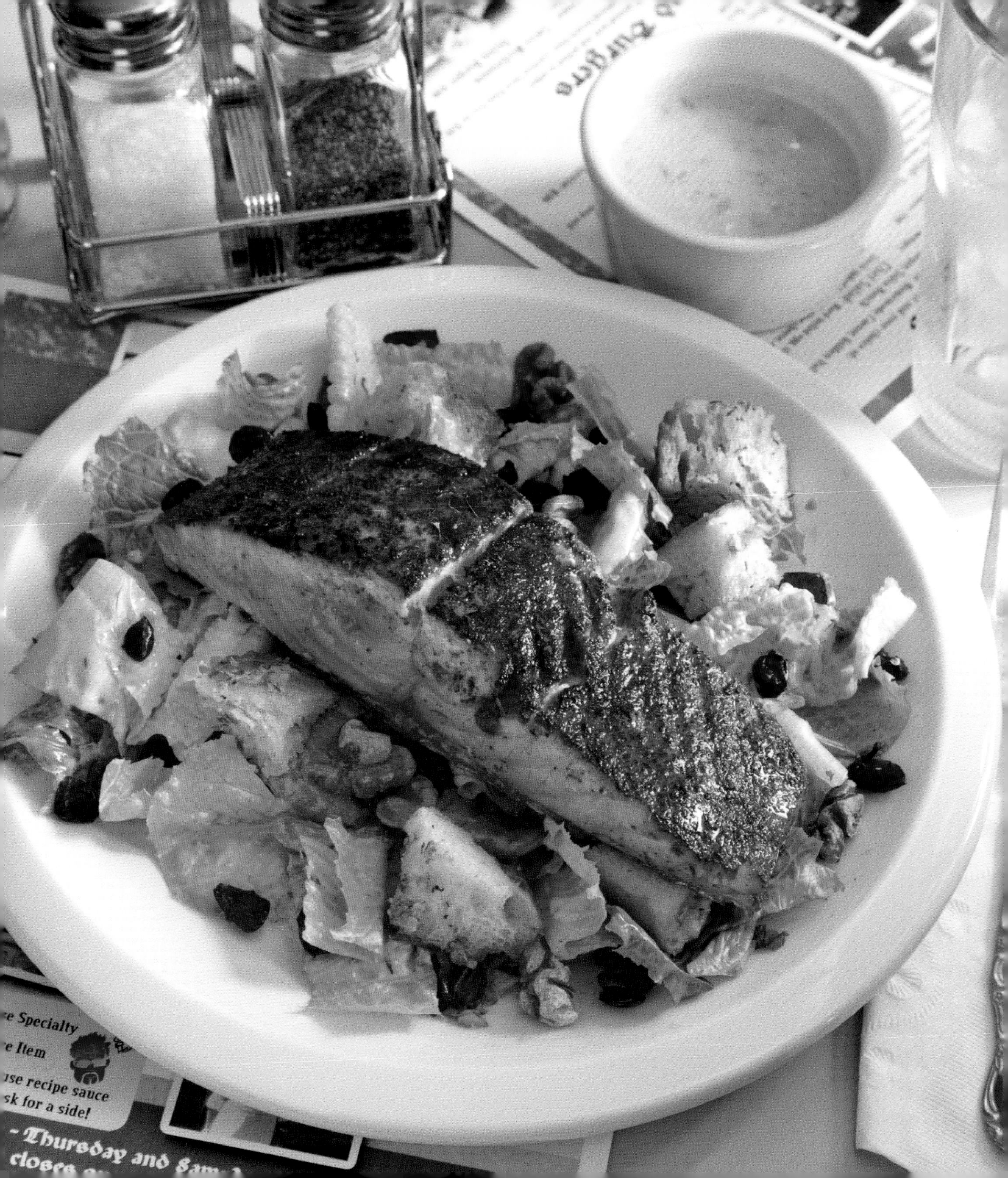
Specialty
Item
recipe sauce
for a side!
Thursday and

Tune Inn's Beer-Battered Flounder Sandwiches

These sandwiches are crispy and not too bready–ideal pub food.

Canola oil

2   cups all-purpose flour
⅓   cup seasoned salt
¼   tsp. paprika
4   cups lager beer
4   (6-oz.) flounder fillets
4   potato rolls or kaiser rolls

Toppings: lettuce leaves, tomato slices, Dijon
          mustard, and mayonnaise

1. Pour oil to depth of 3 inches into a Dutch oven or deep fryer; heat to 350°.
2. Whisk together flour and next 2 ingredients in a large bowl. Whisk in beer until smooth.
3. Dip fillets in batter, allowing excess to drip off. Fry fillets, in batches, 3 minutes or until done. Drain on a wire rack over paper towels. Serve on rolls with desired toppings. **Makes 4 servings.**

Tune Inn

When my Navy shipmate Matt Miller, a Washington, D.C., insider, first told me about the Tune Inn, he simply said, "Morgan, this is your kinda place." When I went inside and saw what appeared to be a taxidermist's office mixed with a Harley dealership, my first thought was, "I guess my house needs a woman's touch." But Matt was right. The Tune Inn is my kinda place. Whereas most of this town is designed to be so grand as to elicit cries of "Holy hair of Ronald Reagan, THIS is where all my tax money went!" the Tune Inn is simple and humble. Don't be fooled, citizen. Decor aside, the food is fantastic, the beer is cold, and the location is perfect. I mean, come on—the address is 331 *and a half* Pennsylvania. That's the kind of insider stuff that Washingtonians love.

Cafe Hon

1002 West 36th Street
Baltimore, Maryland
(410) 243-1230

The giant pink flamingo on the outside of the building will be your first clue: This place is bonkers. Still not convinced? Wander through the gift shop, several hundred square feet filled with brightly colored wigs, zany sunglasses, Natty Boh (National Bohemian) beer collectibles, bumper stickers, and "Bawlmer, Murlin"-themed gifts. Don't get so caught up in the cool stuff that you forget to eat, though. Cafe Hon serves some mean diner food. I love their Thanksgiving dinner—which, being true patriots, they serve every day. (America!) The turkey is nothing short of fabulous. "Hon" is short for "honey," so the restaurant name sounds more like "Cafe Hun." And the big-haired waitresses with the sparkly eyewear do, indeed, call you "honey" when you order.

Cafe Hon's Marinated Turkey Breast

Cafe Hon serves the most tender, juicy turkey breasts I've ever tasted. Their recipe hinges on their secret marinade, which is more like thick vinaigrette.

1½	cups Dijon mustard
1½	cups olive oil
¾	cup red wine vinegar
2	Tbsp. chopped fresh thyme
6	Tbsp. honey
2¼	tsp. salt
1½	tsp. pepper
1	(4-lb.) skin-on, boned turkey breast, halved

1. Whisk together first 7 ingredients in a medium bowl. Place turkey breast halves in a large shallow dish or large zip-top plastic freezer bag. Pour Dijon mixture over turkey, turning to coat. Cover or seal, and chill 24 hours. Remove turkey from marinade, discarding marinade.
2. Preheat oven to 425°. Place turkey on a lightly greased wire rack in a roasting pan. Bake at 425° for 30 minutes; reduce oven temperature to 325°, and bake 40 more minutes or until a meat thermometer registers 165°. Let stand 15 minutes before carving. **Makes 8 servings.**

Note: If you can't find skin-on, boned turkey breast, buy a 5-lb. skin-on, bone-in breast, and ask the butcher to cut it in half lengthwise and remove the bones for you.

Cafe Hon's Turkey Gravy

You can pick the meat from the reserved turkey wings, and add it to the completed gravy, or use it to make turkey salad.

6	(¾-lb.) turkey wings
2	medium onions, peeled and quartered
8	cups chicken broth, divided
I	cup chopped carrots
½	tsp. dried thyme
I	cup all-purpose flour
2½	Tbsp. unsalted butter
½	tsp. salt
½	tsp. pepper

1. Preheat oven to 400°. Arrange turkey wings in a single layer in a lightly greased roasting pan; scatter onions over the wings. Bake at 400° for 1 hour and 10 minutes or until wings and onions are browned.

2. Place wings and onions in a 6- or 8-qt. Dutch oven. Add 1 cup water to the hot roasting pan, scraping up the browned bits on the bottom of the pan. Pour water and browned bits from the roasting pan into Dutch oven. Stir in 6 cups broth, carrots, and thyme. Bring to a boil over high heat. Reduce heat to medium-low, and simmer, uncovered, for 1 hour and 30 minutes or until mixture is reduced by half. (You should have about 4 cups).

3. Remove wings from Dutch oven, and reserve for another use. Pour broth mixture through a wire-mesh strainer into a large saucepan, pressing vegetables gently with the back of a spoon to ensure all liquid is removed. Discard vegetables. Let broth mixture stand 10 minutes; skim fat.

4. Bring broth mixture in saucepan to a boil. Whisk together flour and remaining 2 cups chicken broth in a medium bowl until smooth. Gradually whisk flour mixture into boiling broth mixture. Reduce heat, and simmer, stirring often, 3 minutes or until thickened. Stir in butter, salt, and pepper. Serve immediately. **Makes 6½ cups.**

Cafe Hon's Dressing

This finely textured dressing is part of the everyday Thanksgiving plate at Cafe Hon.

1   turkey liver or 3 chicken livers
1   (1-lb.) package ground pork sage sausage
1   cup finely chopped white onion
¾   cup finely chopped celery
½   tsp. poultry seasoning
1   (14-oz.) bag herb-seasoned stuffing mix
⅓   cup minced fresh parsley
1¾   cups chicken broth
¼   cup unsalted butter, melted

1. Place liver in a small saucepan with water to cover. Bring to a boil, and cook 2 minutes or until done. Drain; cool slightly, and finely chop.

2. Cook sausage and onion in a large skillet over medium heat, stirring often, 10 minutes or until sausage crumbles and is no longer pink. Add celery and poultry seasoning; cook 2 minutes, stirring often, to blend flavors.

3. Preheat oven to 350°. Stir together liver, sausage mixture, stuffing mix, and parsley in a large bowl. Drizzle with chicken broth and butter; stir gently.

4. Spoon dressing into a lightly greased 13- x 9-inch baking dish. Bake, uncovered, at 350° for 30 minutes or until thoroughly heated and top is lightly browned. **Makes 10 servings.**

Note: We tested with Jimmy Dean ground pork sage sausage and Pepperidge Farm herb-seasoned stuffing mix.

Cafe Hon's Cranberry Relish

This very tart relish is a refreshing slap across the tongue and a welcome detour from overly sweet Thanksgiving cranberry sauces.

2   (12-oz.) packages fresh or frozen cranberries, thawed
2   Tbsp. orange zest
1   Tbsp. lime zest
½   cup fresh orange juice
¼   cup fresh lime juice
½   cup firmly packed light brown sugar
½   cup granulated sugar
⅛   tsp. ground cloves

1. Process cranberries in a food processor 30 seconds or until finely chopped, stopping to scrape down sides.

2. Stir together zests, juices, sugars, and cloves in a large bowl. Stir in cranberries. **Makes 4 cups.**

The Crab Claw Restaurant

304 Burns Street
St. Michaels, Maryland
(410) 745-2900

Wooden picnic tables and waterfront dining have made the Crab Claw a Maryland classic since 1965. Open from March through December, this sprawling restaurant serves beautiful blue crabs and Maryland standards such as Crab Imperial. First time eating crab? Grab a bib, look at your place mat, and follow the simple instructions. You'll be a crab-slaughtering master in no time flat. You can also ask a member of the helpful wait staff for a tutorial. How to spot an old-timer here? Look for anyone with a house account for beer and crustaceans.

Crab Claw Cocktail Sauce

This beloved recipe is incredibly simple. You'll wonder why you ever buy it in a jar.

1	cup ketchup
1	cup refrigerated horseradish
¼	tsp. fresh lemon juice
⅛	tsp. Old Bay seasoning

1. Stir together all ingredients in a small bowl. Makes 2 cups.

Crab Claw Crab Imperial

Warm and dense, this Eastern Shore favorite isn't a dip. It's typically served as an appetizer or side dish, and eaten with a fork.

2	lb. fresh jumbo lump crabmeat, drained
1	cup mayonnaise
¼	tsp. dried parsley
¼	tsp. Old Bay seasoning
¼	tsp. dry mustard
⅛	tsp. fresh lemon juice
1	large egg, beaten

1. Preheat oven to 400°. Pick through crabmeat, removing any shell. Stir together mayonnaise and next 5 ingredients in a bowl; stir in crabmeat.
2. Divide crab mixture into lightly greased (1-cup) scallop shells or baking dishes. Bake, uncovered, at 400° for 25 minutes or until tops are golden. **Makes 6 servings.**

Note: To make one family-style dish, prepare as directed in Step 1. Spoon crab mixture into an 8- x 8-inch baking dish. Bake, uncovered, at 400°

Main Ingredient Snickerdoodle French Toast

The crispy bits on the crust of this French toast will make you think it has a bit of chocolate, even though it doesn't. Buy an oblong loaf of brioche, rather than a round one, for uniform slices.

1	(1-lb.) oblong loaf brioche (about 8 inches)
6	large eggs
1½	cups milk
1	tsp. ground cinnamon
2	tsp. vanilla extract

Pinch of salt

1	cup sugar
1	Tbsp. ground cinnamon

Butter

Syrup

Garnishes: fresh raspberries, powdered sugar

1. Cut bread into 8 (1-inch-thick) slices. Whisk together eggs and next 4 ingredients in a large bowl. Stir together sugar and cinnamon in a small bowl. Quickly dip bread slices, 1 at a time, into egg mixture, coating both sides of bread. Place bread on a baking sheet; sprinkle half of cinnamon-sugar over tops of bread slices.
2. Melt a dollop of butter in a large skillet over medium heat. Add half of bread slices, cinnamon-sugar side down, to skillet; sprinkle tops of bread slices with cinnamon-sugar. Cook 2 minutes on each side or until egg mixture is set and a crispy crust forms on bread. Transfer to a baking sheet; keep warm in a 300° oven. Repeat procedure with remaining bread slices and cinnamon-sugar, adding more butter to skillet as needed. Serve with butter and your favorite syrup. **Makes 4 servings.**

The Main Ingredient

914 Bay Ridge Road
Annapolis, Maryland
(410) 626-0388

Say you're a Navy midshipman just off the boat in Annapolis, and you want to take your mama to lunch. You could go to a saloon; Annapolis brims with old watering holes. But the thought of your dear mama in a bar is more unsettling than losing a game to Army—and yet, you don't have the cash for a fancy-pants spot. Where to go? The Main Ingredient. It's in a strip mall and rather unassuming. Inside, you'll find fabulous fare at reasonable prices. My favorite dish, the Hungarian mushroom soup, may sound a tad odd, but believe me, you'll be glad you ordered it. And if you're a breakfast fan, you can't go wrong with the French toast—crusty as an old admiral and sweet as three days of shore leave.

Main Ingredient
Hungarian Mushroom Soup

This soup is rich and creamy, with a pleasant lift from paprika and dill.

1	cup unsalted butter
½	cup finely chopped onion
2	Tbsp. dried dill weed
2	Tbsp. sweet paprika
1	cup all-purpose flour
2	qt. beef broth
2½	lb. sliced fresh mushrooms
2	tsp. salt
1	tsp. freshly ground pepper
2	cups heavy cream
2	cups sour cream

Bread and butter

Garnishes: sour cream, fresh dill weed

1. Melt butter in a 6-qt. Dutch oven over medium-high heat. Add onion, and sauté 5 minutes. Add dill and paprika; sauté 1 minute. Reduce heat to medium-low. Sprinkle flour over butter mixture, whisking until smooth. Cook 15 minutes, whisking occasionally.

2. Gradually add beef broth, whisking until blended. Add mushrooms, salt, and pepper. Reduce heat to low, and cook, uncovered, 40 minutes or until thickened, stirring often. Remove from heat, and let cool 15 minutes.

3. Whisk together heavy cream and sour cream in a large bowl. Gradually stir about one-fourth of warm mushroom mixture into sour cream mixture; add sour cream mixture to remaining warm mushroom mixture in Dutch over, stirring constantly. Cook over low heat 5 minutes or until thoroughly heated, stirring often. Ladle soup into bowls. Serve with bread and butter.
Makes 15 cups.

SOUNDTRACK:

"Public Service Announcement" by The Bravery (lead singer, Sam Endicott, is from the Bethesda area)

"Dream a Little Dream of Me" by Maryland native Mama Cass Elliot of the Mamas and the Papas

"Minnie the Moocher" by Baltimore son Cab Calloway

"Only Wanna Be With You" by Hootie & the Blowfish

"Let's Do It" by Baltimore grand dame Billie Holiday

Out of the Fire Goat Cheese Salad

Hearty and tangy, it's perfect for a light lunch.

Cheese

1	(½-oz.) slice French bread, torn in large pieces
½	cup walnuts
1	(4-oz.) goat cheese log, cut into 6 slices
2	Tbsp. olive oil
¼	cup canola oil

Dressing

½	cup extra virgin olive oil
¼	cup lemon juice (about 3 lemons)
1	tsp. minced fresh thyme
1	tsp. Dijon mustard
½	tsp. salt
½	tsp. freshly ground pepper

Salad

½	cup sliced baby portobello mushrooms
½	tsp. Za'atar seasoning
¾	cup thinly sliced sweet onion
½	cup oil-cured olives, pitted and sliced
1	(14-oz.) can quartered artichoke hearts, drained
2	(5-oz.) packages arugula

1. Prepare Cheese: Pulse bread in a food processor until coarse crumbs form; add walnuts, and process until finely ground. Brush cheese slices with 2 Tbsp. olive oil; dredge in walnut mixture, pressing to adhere. Place slices in a small baking pan. Freeze 30 minutes.
2. Heat canola oil in a skillet over medium-low heat. Remove cheese from freezer. Cook cheese slices in hot oil 1½ to 2 minutes on each side or until browned and crisp. Drain on paper towels.
3. Prepare Dressing: Place all ingredients in a 1-pt. jar; cover with a tight-fitting lid, and shake vigorously until blended.

Out of the Fire

22 Goldsborough Street
Easton, Maryland
(410) 770-4777

Along the charming brick streets of one of the Eastern Shore's most beautiful towns, Out of the Fire beckons diners searching for something a little upscale but not pretentious. Owner Amy Haines started the restaurant after leaving corporate America (hence the name, "Out of the Fire"), and the creative result blossomed into a local favorite. With a range that runs from oyster pot pie to wood-fired pizza, the menu says "Maryland" without clocking you over the noggin with a crab mallet.

4. Prepare Salad: Place mushrooms in a large bowl; sprinkle with Za'atar seasoning, and toss well. Add onion and next 3 ingredients; drizzle with dressing, and toss to coat. Divide among serving bowls, and top with cheese slices. **Makes 6 servings.**

Out of the Fire Mussels

These mussels get their smoke-tinged flavor from the amazing roasted sauce, a go-to recipe that can also be used as a dipping sauce for bread, a pizza topping, and a pasta sauce.

1   cup Chardonnay or other dry white wine
½   cup bottled clam juice
⅓   cup drained capers
2   Tbsp. extra virgin olive oil
2   tsp. dried crushed red pepper
⅛   tsp. black pepper
16 garlic cloves, chopped
2   lb. fresh mussels, scrubbed and debearded
1   cup Roasted Pizza Sauce (at right)
Grilled bread
Garnish: sliced green onions

1. Combine first 7 ingredients in a 6-qt. Dutch oven. Add mussels. Cover; cook over high heat 3 minutes or until mussels open. (Discard any unopened mussels.)
2. Stir in 1 cup Roasted Pizza Sauce, and serve immediately with grilled bread. **Makes 4 servings.**

Roasted Pizza Sauce

4   (28-oz.) cans plum tomatoes
⅓   cup extra virgin olive oil
⅓   cup chopped onion
12 garlic cloves, chopped
⅓   cup chopped sun-dried tomatoes
2   Tbsp. sugar
3   Tbsp. chopped fresh basil
3   Tbsp. chopped fresh oregano
1   tsp. salt
1   tsp. freshly ground pepper

1. Preheat oven to 450°. Drain tomatoes, reserving tomatoes and 1¾ cups juice; place in a large bowl. Crush tomatoes, using clean hands or a potato masher.
2. Heat oil in a 16- x 12-inch roasting pan over medium-high heat, swirling to coat bottom of pan. Add onion; sauté 2 minutes or until tender. Add garlic; sauté 30 seconds. Stir in sun-dried tomatoes, next 5 ingredients, and crushed tomato mixture.
3. Bake, uncovered, at 450° for 1 hour or until thickened. Increase oven temperature to broil. Broil 5½ inches from heat 8 minutes or until top is charred. **Makes 6½ cups.**

Note: Sauce may be made ahead, chilled, and frozen in zip-top plastic freezer bags or freezer containers up to 3 months. Thaw in refrigerator, and heat thoroughly before using.

OVERHEARD: "I'm chockablock."

I like to use this old nautical expression when I've eaten myself silly, which is easy to do in Mary's land. It comes from the point in sailing when the ropes are pulled so tight the tackle's chock meets the block, so the literal meaning is "taut" or "out of slack."

Out of the Fire Oyster Pot Pies

At the restaurant, these rich, individual pot pies are topped with a cream-cheese dough. We made them a smidge faster but no less indulgent with ready-made piecrust dough.

3	bacon slices
1¼	cups diced carrot
1	cup chopped onion
1	cup diced celery
¼	cup butter
⅓	cup all-purpose flour
2	cups half-and-half
1½	cups diced unpeeled baking potato
1	tsp. salt
1	tsp. freshly ground pepper
¼	cup Spanish sherry
1	Tbsp. chopped fresh thyme
1	(16-oz.) container oysters, drained
1	(14.1-oz.) package refrigerated piecrusts
2	Tbsp. extra virgin olive oil

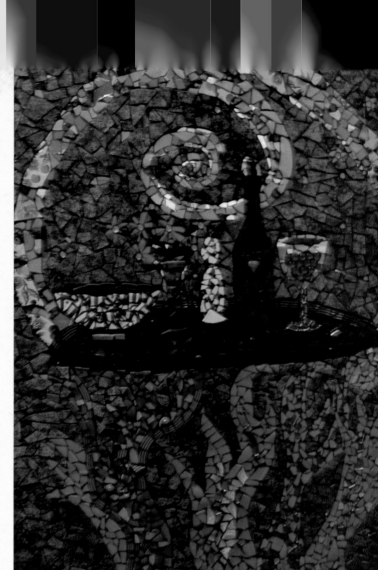

1. Preheat oven to 450°. Cook bacon in a large skillet 5 minutes or until crisp; remove bacon, reserving 1 Tbsp. drippings in pan. Crumble bacon. Cook carrot and next 2 ingredients in hot drippings 8 minutes or until tender. Remove from heat.

2. Melt butter in a heavy saucepan over low heat; whisk in flour until smooth. Cook 1 minute, whisking constantly. Gradually whisk in half-and-half and next 3 ingredients; cook over medium heat 4 minutes, whisking constantly, until mixture is thickened and bubbly. Stir in sherry and thyme. Stir potato mixture into vegetable mixture.

3. Divide vegetable mixture evenly among 4 lightly greased (2-cup) crocks. Place one-fourth of the oysters (9 to 10 oysters) in each crock; stir oysters into vegetable mixture.

4. Roll each piecrust into an 11-inch circle on a lightly floured surface. Cut 2 (5-inch) circles from each piecrust. Place circles on top of filling in crocks. Cut slits in crust to let steam escape.

5. Brush crusts with olive oil. Bake at 450° for 30 minutes or until crust is browned and filling is bubbly. Let stand 5 minutes before serving. **Makes 4 servings.**

Papermoon Diner

227 West 29th Street
Baltimore, Maryland
(410) 889-4444

Iridescent mannequins and roses growing out of toilet bowls welcome guests to my favorite gem in Baltimore. Inside, the Papermoon Diner overflows with stuff: Pez dispensers, Legos, old dolls, rotary phones, signage from decades past, and toys that you probably owned as a child. Everyone, at some point during their meal, will point at a wall and say, "Hey, I used to have one of those!" The original diner seats 13, though there are now two small additional dining rooms where you can order a honey-ginger or bacon-chocolate milk shake (trust me, you'll love it), and let out your inner weirdo over masterful dishes such as salmon burgers and sausage bread pudding. The food is just as unusual as the decor, but somehow, like an alien mannequin covered in rhinestones, it just works.

Papermoon Sausage Bread Pudding

This savory-sweet dish is the culinary equivalent of dunking your sausage in pancake syrup.

1 lb. ground pork sausage
10 cups (1-inch) Challah bread cubes
6 large eggs
1 qt. half-and-half
1½ cups milk
3 Tbsp. butter, melted
1 tsp. kosher salt
1 tsp. pepper
Pinch of ground nutmeg
3 cups (12 oz.) shredded Cheddar cheese
2 Tbsp. powdered sugar
Maple syrup, warmed

1. Brown sausage in a large skillet over medium-high heat, stirring often, 5 to 8 minutes or until sausage crumbles and is no longer pink; drain. Remove sausage from skillet using a slotted spoon; drain on paper towels.

2. Place bread cubes in a lightly greased 13-x 9-inch baking dish. Whisk together eggs and next 6 ingredients in a large bowl. Pour egg mixture over bread. Top with sausage, pressing into egg mixture. Sprinkle with cheese. Cover with aluminum foil, and chill 8 hours.

3. Remove from refrigerator, and let stand at room temperature 1 hour.

4. Preheat oven to 325°. Bake, covered, at 325° for 45 minutes. Uncover and bake 15 more minutes or until lightly browned. Cool on a wire rack 30 minutes. Sprinkle with powdered sugar. Cut into squares. Serve with maple syrup. **Makes 12 servings.**

www.papermoondiner24.com

Papermoon Salmon Burgers

Imagine your favorite crab cake. Now send it to Asia and the Mediterranean, use salmon instead of crab, and park it on a Maryland bun, and you'll have something close to this burger. Zesty sambal oelek, briny olive mayonnaise, and sweet roasted peppers combine in unexpected ways to take these toothsome patties—and you—over the moon.

2	large eggs
¼	cup mayonnaise
2	Tbsp. chopped fresh cilantro
1	Tbsp. fresh lemon juice
1	Tbsp. soy sauce
2	tsp. Dijon mustard
2	tsp. sambal oelek (ground fresh chile paste)
1½	tsp. chopped green onions
¼	tsp. salt
1¼	lbs. skinless salmon fillet, pin bones removed, cut into ½-inch pieces
½	cup panko (Japanese breadcrumbs)
6	kaiser rolls, split and toasted

Olive Aioli (at right)
Toppings: arugula or baby spinach, and roasted red pepper slices

1. Whisk together first 9 ingredients in a large bowl. Gently fold in salmon and panko. Shape mixture by ½ cupfuls into 4-inch patties; place on a wax paper-lined baking sheet.
2. Cook patties, in batches, in a lightly greased large cast-iron skillet over medium-high heat 3 minutes on each side or until lightly browned and desired degree of doneness.
3. Serve on kaiser rolls with Olive Aioli and desired toppings. **Makes 6 servings.**

Olive Aioli

½	cup finely chopped pitted kalamata olives
½	cup mayonnaise
2	Tbsp. olive oil
1	tsp. drained capers
½	tsp. minced garlic

1. Stir together all ingredients in a small bowl. Cover and chill until ready to serve. **Makes about 1 cup.**

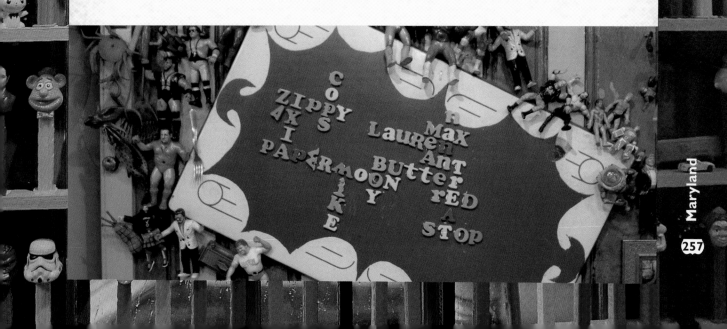

Papermoon Honey-Ginger Shakes

Sweet and spicy, peppery and cold, these are the yin and yang of shakes.

- 1   cup finely chopped fresh ginger
- ½   cup honey
- ¼   cup sugar
- 1   Tbsp. fresh lemon juice
- 4   cups vanilla ice cream

Sweetened whipped cream

1. Combine first 4 ingredients and 2 Tbsp. water in a saucepan. Bring to a boil; reduce heat, and simmer, uncovered, 10 minutes. Remove from heat, and let stand 15 minutes. Pour through a fine wire-mesh strainer into a bowl; discard solids. Let syrup cool completely.

2. Combine syrup and ice cream in a blender; process until smooth. Pour into glasses; top with dollops of whipped cream. Serve immediately.

Makes 4 cups.

Papermoon Diner

Papermoon looks to have been designed by Lady Gaga on an acid-and-eBay bender. I'm trying to come up with a word for the result. Clutterific? Toytastic? My favorite restaurant in Maryland is, as my English friends would say, mad but brilliant. Use a potty as a planter and decorate with Star Wars figurines? Why not? Pass the Pez and gin! Sometimes you need a little bit of crazy to come up with something truly groundbreaking—like the sausage bread pudding. Anyone can bake a turkey. But putting two breakfast dishes together? Who would have thought? A drugged-up lady in a bacon dress, that's who. But also the folks at Papermoon.

Maryland

Kearney
Lincoln
Hastings
Beatrice
Peoria
Washington
Normal
Bloomington
Champaign
Urbana
Danville
Lafayette
West Lafayette
Kokomo
Muncie
Indiana
Indianapolis
Anderson
Columbus
Dayton
Springfield
Xenia
Kettering
Hamilton
Cincinnati
Fort Madison
Burlington
Keokuk
Macomb
Quincy
Springfield
Illinois
Decatur
Terre Haute
Missouri
Saint Joseph
Hannibal
Kirksville
Moberly
Columbia
Mexico
Kansas City
Independence
Overland Park
Olathe
Topeka
Manhattan
Junction City
Salina
Hays
Kansas
McPherson
Hutchinson
Great Bend
Dodge City
Wichita
El Dorado
Emporia
Lawrence
Jefferson City
Saint Peters
Saint Charles
Saint Louis
Wildwood
Washington
Fulton
Sedalia
Rolla
Farmington
Carbondale
Centralia
Mount Vernon
Evansville
Owensboro
Louisville
Frankfort
Lexington
Richmond
Berea
Danville
Elizabethtown
Bowling Green
Kentucky
Paducah
Cape Girardeau
Sikeston
Poplar Bluff
West Plains
Springfield
Joplin
Branson
Coffeyville
Arkansas City
Ponca City
Bartlesville
Enid
Stillwater
Owasso
Tulsa
Broken Arrow
Claremore
Bixby
Sapulpa
Muskogee
Tahlequah
Okmulgee
Oklahoma
Edmond
Oklahoma City
Midwest City
Moore
Norman
Shawnee
Chickasha
Lawton
Ada
McAlester
Ardmore
Durant
Wichita Falls
Denton
Sherman
Rogers
Bentonville
Springdale
Fayetteville
Harrison
Mountain Home
Fort Smith
Van Buren
Russellville
Conway
Searcy
Jonesboro
Blytheville
Arkansas
North Little Rock
Little Rock
Jacksonville
Cabot
Hot Springs
Benton
Pine Bluff
Stuttgart
Arkadelphia
Camden
El Dorado
Magnolia
Texarkana
West Memphis
Memphis
Collierville
Southaven
Horn Lake
Dyersburg
Jackson
Union City
Clarksville
Nashville
Murfreesboro
Franklin
Columbia
Tennessee
Cookeville
Knoxville
Oak Ridge
Johnson City
Kingsport
Morristown
Maryville
Dayton
Athens
Cleveland
Chattanooga
Dalton
Huntsville
Decatur
Florence
Corinth
Tupelo
Oxford
Clarksdale
Cleveland
Greenwood
Grenada
Columbus
Starkville
Mississippi
Greenville
Yazoo City
Jackson
Vicksburg
Meridian
Hattiesburg
Laurel
Tuscaloosa
Birmingham
Hoover
Gadsden
Anniston
Rome
Marietta
Roswell
Atlanta
Kennesaw
Gainesville
Peachtree City
Griffin
LaGrange
Auburn
Opelika
Columbus
Montgomery
Alabama
Selma
Dothan
Albany
Georgia
Tallahassee
Mobile
Fairhope
Bay Minette
Saraland
Pensacola
Destin
Niceville
Crestview
Panama City
Lynn Haven
Biloxi
Gulfport
Pascagoula
Slidell
Hammond
Baton Rouge
Lafayette
Lake Charles
New Iberia
Houma
Thibodaux
Kenner
New Orleans
Louisiana
Alexandria
Natchitoches
Shreveport
Bossier City
Monroe
Ruston
Longview
Tyler
Texarkana
Dallas
Plano
Garland
Irving
Carrollton
Fort Worth
Arlington
Abilene
Waco
Killeen
Temple
Belton
Georgetown
Round Rock
Austin
Bryan
College Station
Huntsville
Conroe
Beaumont
Port Arthur
Orange
Houston
Sugar Land
Pasadena
Baytown
Galveston
San Marcos
New Braunfels
San Antonio
Victoria
Corpus Christi
Kingsville
Laredo
McAllen
Edinburg
Harlingen
Brownsville

WHERE to REST YOUR HEAD

Best Hotels, Resorts, and Inns Across the South

One of the best words in the English language? Housekeeping. Does there exist anything quite so wonderful as a bed that someone else makes or a fluffy towel set out for you by another? Yes, indeedy, I love a fabulous hotel, a quirky motel, a quaint historic inn, and even the average bed-and-breakfast (minus the cats and little toilet doilies, of course).

I've traveled a lot and been in more hotel rooms than the Gideon Bible, so I know what makes a great place to kick up your feet, which spots will be the most memorable, and where you'll be pampered like a distinguished guest.

Selecting the right spot hinges on your budget and taste, of course. But there are a few universal rules about where to lay your head. First, if it's a run-of-the-mill trip, opt for clean and safe. That's easy (and, for me, usually a Hampton Inn). Second, if you're looking to spend the night somewhere special, to learn about a new town, to celebrate an anniversary or special occasion, you owe it to yourself to pick a hotel that speaks to where you are, a place that reflects the local flavor. Third, it's not a crime to pay more for a hotel from time to time, as long as it's worth the splurge.

In researching this book and its precursor, the original *Off the Eaten Path*, I stayed at hotels across the South. These are my very favorites in each state. Even though they have vastly different price points, each offers what I consider a good value.

Alabama

The Grand Hotel
1 Grand Boulevard, Point Clear
(251) 928-9201 $$

My grandmother Edwina used to say, "You can't carry anything bigger than a pocketbook across the lobby of The Grand." It's true. The attentive staff and elegant grounds make this venerable Alabama classic a spot worth visiting. Many fine families from the Heart of Dixie have made The Grand an annual visit for generations. Relax in the spa, fish off the

dock, park it on the beach, visit nearby Fort Morgan, tour the battleship USS *Alabama*, or go explore quaint Fairhope. It's all convenient from The Grand. Don't feel like going out? Simply kick back in the lobby and get to know the other guests. This hotel fosters an easy camaraderie like no other.

Arkansas

The Capital Hotel
111 West Markham Street, Little Rock
(501) 374-7474 $$

Talk about elegance. This stunningly restored hotel, in the heart of downtown Little Rock, boasts Gilded-Age style, modern convenience, and a staff that ranks nothing short of exceptional. Take the elevator, for instance: It's large enough to accommodate a guest and his horse, in case you were thinking of bringing Trigger. Likewise, the hotel's 94 rooms are huge—not the cramped variety you find in

most historic hotels. The Capital Bar & Grill remains a swank spot to have a cocktail, and I love sitting out on the comfortable porches. That reminds me how the hotel got its name: an early patron remarked that the spot was "a capital enterprise located in a capital building." And staying here on your next visit to Arkansas is a capital idea.

District of Columbia

The Jefferson
1200 Sixteenth Street Northwest, Washington
(202) 448-2300 $$$$

This Beaux-Arts hotel within spitting distance of the White House (Note: Do not spit on the president's home. Thanks, Mgmt.) charms guests with all sorts of Jeffersonian touches. The classical lobby, designed by French architect Jules de Sibour, has a sophisticated feel. Busts of the founding father, along with many documents bearing his signature, decorate the public spaces. The former president would have adored the Book Room, an intimate spot to retreat and browse signed copies by authors who have stayed in the hotel. (Yep, *Off the Eaten Path* is in there.) The elegantly appointed rooms make every guest feel like a Washington power broker, but if you can't afford to stay overnight, hang out at the bar. It's framed by celestial maps and boasts a collection of Madeira wines. Old T.J. would have approved, for sure.

Price Guide: *Hotel rates vary by season, day of the week, and what's going on in town. Still, on average, for each dollar symbol listed, you can assume about $100 for the nightly tab on a double-occupancy room. Want a bargain? Ask for off-season dates, check for discounts, and join the hotel's email list. Often the best rates go to the most loyal customers.*

Florida

The Coral Gables Biltmore Hotel
1200 Anastasia Avenue, Coral Gables
(855) 311-6903 $$

I could be wearing a white dinner jacket and still feel underdressed in the lobby of the Biltmore. There's just something about the elegance of the setting that seems at odds with our flip-flops-and-fanny-pack culture. Is this a hotel or the palace of some Venetian prince? Frescos grace the ceilings. The travertine floors sparkle. Leaded glass and mahogany abound. Stay at the Biltmore, and you'll be treading in the footsteps of the Duke and Duchess of Windsor, Bobby Jones, Al Capone, and just about every star of the 20th century. It's that kind of hotel. But more than history, this Miami institution boasts a spectacular golf course, spa, and pool where you'll want to while away an entire day in South Florida's sunny weather. The Coral Gables Biltmore remains a resort in the oldest and grandest sense of the word. It's worth a splurge.

Georgia

Barnsley Gardens Resort
597 Barnsley Gardens Road, Adairsville
(877) 773-2447 $$$

In my favorite Bible verse, Adam and Eve hear the voice of the Lord "walking in the garden in the cool of the afternoon." If the best gardens are places of love, peace, and heavenly reflection, Barnsley Gardens boasts one of the most divine gardens in the

South. The Georgia resort was built on the ruins of a 19th-century plantation destroyed during the War Between the States, or the "late unpleasantness," as my grandmother called it. There's nothing quite so romantic as the decayed elegance here. The sophisticated rooms, suites, English cottages, and lush 3,300 acres are an intoxicating setting for a couple's weekend escape. Barnsley offers tennis, golf, a European-style spa, shooting, hunting, horseback riding, and the services of a "fairy godmother," who sets up dinners and jaunts fit for a storybook. It's all just 60 miles north of Atlanta.

Kentucky

A Storybook Inn
277 Rose Hill Avenue, Versailles
(859) 879-9993 $$$

Right in the heart of horse country sits one of my favorite bed-and-breakfast inns. The main house, which dates to the 1830s, certainly lends itself to being a hotel. The large rooms give a sense of privacy that many B&Bs lack. Each is decorated in the style of a classic movie, such as *Gone with the Wind* and *African Queen*. Innkeeper Elise Buckley is an old-house person—and also a terrific cook—so touring the property and feasting on her breakfasts is well worth a trip. Rooms book up fast, especially around major horse events, so make sure to call in advance.

Louisiana
The Roosevelt Hotel
123 Baronne Street, New Orleans
(504) 648-1200 $$

During the 1960s, my favorite aunt couldn't afford to stay here—but she did visit the hotel's legendary bar, the Sazerac, and nursed a drink for hours just to take in the place. When I told Auntie Peggy I splurged for a weekend at the Roosevelt, she waxed at length about the hotel's staff, the unforgettable tile lobby, and the romantic setting—all just steps from the French Quarter. "Is the old girl still the same?" she asked. Better, I'd say. Hilton recently spent $200 million to restore the Grande Dame de NOLA to her former glory. From John Besh's new restaurant in the lobby to the rooms' super-comfy beds, the Roosevelt offers an unforgettable dose of the Big Easy.

Maryland
The Inn at Perry Cabin
308 Watkins Lane, St. Michaels
(410) 745-2200 $$$$

The first time I set foot in the charming town of St. Michaels, I fell in love with its quaint, history-steeped downtown. During the War of 1812, the villagers hoisted lanterns into the trees one night to throw off the Brits. The Royal Navy cannons overshot the town, and St. Michaels has hence been known as the "town that fooled the British." Likewise, the elegant Inn at Perry Cabin is awash with history. Built by an aide to Naval Commodore Oliver Hazard Perry, the manor house has many nautical nods. The rooms are spectacular (many have stunning views of the water), and the restaurant

and grounds are not to be missed, even if you just visit for the day. The polished brass, gleaming wood, crisp white linens, and deep navy blues of the inn's decor will turn even the most dedicated land-lubber into a lover of the sea.

Mississippi
The Alluvian Hotel
318 Howard Street, Greenwood
(866) 600-5201 $

Finding The Alluvian Hotel in Greenwood is like stumbling over a unicorn in Grand Central Station. Whoa, unicorn! How did you get here? The Alluvian is a posh luxury hotel that I'd expect to find in London. Not that Greenwood isn't a neat place to visit. However, London it ain't (a fact you'll be grateful for when you get the bill). The Alluvian's rooms are modern and spacious. The stylish lobby is elegant and often filled with music from local bands. And if you want a taste of London, hop into the Alluvian's English cab and get whisked around in British style. Like everything about this Mississippi hotel, it's first class.

Missouri
Hermann Hill
711 Wein Street, Hermann
(573) 486-4455 $

I probably need only four words to convince you Hermann Hill is a superior bed-and-breakfast inn: It's in a vineyard. The original inn (there are also cottages in town) sits atop a gorgeous crest, overlooking downtown Hermann and neat rows of Norton grapes. Turn on your in-room fireplace, grab a glass of wine, and maybe sink into the enormous tub that graces each room. Hermann Hill is a spot where you can

definitely relax. While the inn's decor and common spaces don't have the grandeur of many of the other hotels on this list, the breathtaking panorama it affords of Missouri's Red River Valley includes a light show each sunrise and sunset that no twinkling chandelier or fancy lobby can match.

North Carolina

Mast Farm Inn
2543 Broadstone Road, Banner Elk
(828) 963-5857 $

If you took a cabin in the woods—the serenity, the peaceful natural setting, the moss and trees and whole singing chorus of birds and frogs, and so forth—and then mixed in luxurious linens and first-class service, you'd have Mast Farm Inn. This historic spot, which has welcomed guests since the 1800s, is a tucked-away forest treasure. The inn, which boasts rates as low as $99, can't be beat. I adore their rooms, suites, and cabins. But they also have an award-winning restaurant, Simplicity, that attracts diners from states away. You can visit Mast Farm, have a scrumptious dinner, enjoy a bottle of wine, then fall into your plush bed for a mountain slumber like no other.

Oklahoma

The Mayo Hotel
115 West Fifth Street, Tulsa
(918) 582-6296 $

A wrecking ball nearly destroyed this Tulsa landmark, a fact you'll struggle to believe when you see its opulent lobby (it looks like an MGM movie set) and spacious rooms. Speaking of stars: Big ones—from Bob Hope to Will Rogers—have stayed here. I feel like a star, too, whenever I visit. The sensation begins in the lobby and extends to the brass-lined terrazzo floor and enormous chandeliers of the Crystal Ball-

room. As you'd expect from a recent $40 million renovation, the rooms are modern and fresh. The roof, whose Mayo sign is perhaps the most iconic in all of Tulsa, is a great place to take a guest for a drink. The views are simply stunning.

South Carolina

HarbourView Inn
2 Vendue Range Street, Charleston
(843) 853-8439 $$

Talk about being in the thick of things. HarbourView Inn is downtown's only waterfront hotel and sits just steps from Charleston's City Market, the antiques of King Street, and many of my favorite restaurants. The building itself is historic, but all the rooms are new, quiet, and richly appointed with British flair, as you might expect in this town of Anglophiles. In true Charleston style, they have daily silver service coffee and tea. Make sure to order breakfast, and eat it out on the terrace overlooking Charleston Harbor.

Tennessee

Blackberry Farm
1471 West Millers Cove Road,
Walland
(865) 984-8166 $$$$

If you asked me whether I'd prefer to spend a week on a cruise or two nights at this resort in the hills, I'd pick Blackberry Farm every time. Porters, maids, and waiters run around this place like ticks on a hound. You won't lift a finger from the moment you drive in the front gate. Though it is expensive, Blackberry is not precious or pretentious. There's a real farm feel to staying here. The meals, too, are unforgettable. The folks at this farm are as passionate about food as I am, or maybe more so. Take a cooking class. Go on a picnic. Try fly-fishing lessons. Indulge in the spa. I promise you'll have a good time. And more than that, you'll want to come back regularly.

Texas

The Heywood Hotel
1609 East Cesar Chavez Street, Austin
(512) 271-5522 $$

Heading to the San Francisco of Texas? You've gotta stay someplace cool. Don't settle for some stuffy swank hotel (unless, that is, you're a stuffy politico or the like). I mean, if you're here for the music and food scene—and if you're not, you should be—the place to stay is The Heywood. With just seven rooms it's by far the smallest hotel on this list. But what it lacks in size, it makes up for in fabulousness. The owners have applied a modern aesthetic to what used to be just another old house in the neighborhood. It's sorta like George and Judy Jetson renovated a bungalow. The staff is incredibly helpful. They'll make sure you find what you're looking for in Austin, whether it's vintage boots or an obscure local band playing the night you stay.

Virginia

The Clifton Inn
1296 Clifton Inn Drive, Charlottesville
(434) 971-1800 $$

You can't swing a tricorn hat in Virginia without hitting some fascinating bit of American history, and the site of Charlottesville's Clifton Inn is no exception. These 100 acres of romantic countryside once belonged to Thomas Jefferson's father. Nestled in the Blue Ridge, this columned Southern setting isn't a musty-crusty-rusty retreat. You'll find wireless Internet access, Bose sound systems, Molton Brown soaps and shampoos, and plush Italian linens. Each room is different, and the Clifton boasts walking trails, tennis courts, a croquet lawn, an infinity pool, and convenience to nearby Charlottesville. If you can, time your stay to coincide with one of the inn's incredible multicourse tasting dinners.

West Virginia

The Greenbrier
300 West Main Street, White Sulphur Springs
(855) 453-4858 $$

Since the 18th century, guests have ventured here to "take the waters" for healing purposes. On what was a simple springhouse grew a massive resort, many cottages, and even a bunker to house the federal government in case of nuclear holocaust. (You know a hotel is pretty good when politicians say, "Yep, that's where I want to go for the end of the world.") The Greenbrier has hosted 26 presidents, lots of royalty, and was even where General Robert E. Lee penned the White Sulphur Manifesto. Today, guests can gamble, bowl, shoot pool, fish, hunt, engage in falconry, play laser tag, take a sleigh or carriage ride, golf, bike, kayak, or any number of other activities at the famous resort. It's without a doubt West Virginia's most acclaimed travel destination.

Metric Equivalents

The recipes that appear in this cookbook use the standard U.S. method for measuring liquid and dry or solid ingredients (teaspoons, tablespoons, and cups). The information in the following charts is provided to help cooks outside the United States successfully use these recipes. All equivalents are approximate.

Metric Equivalents for Different Types of Ingredients

A standard cup measure of a dry or solid ingredient will vary in weight depending on the type of ingredient. A standard cup of liquid is the same volume for any type of liquid. Use the following chart when converting standard cup measures to grams (weight) or milliliters (volume).

Standard Cup	Fine Powder (ex. flour)	Grain (ex. rice)	Granular (ex. sugar)	Liquid Solids (ex. butter)	Liquid (ex. milk)
1	140 g	150 g	190 g	200 g	240 ml
¾	105 g	113 g	143 g	150 g	180 ml
⅔	93 g	100 g	125 g	133 g	160 ml
½	70 g	75 g	95 g	100 g	120 ml
⅓	47 g	50 g	63 g	67 g	80 ml
¼	35 g	38 g	48 g	50 g	60 ml
⅛	18 g	19 g	24 g	25 g	30 ml

Useful Equivalents for Dry Ingredients by Weight

(To convert ounces to grams, multiply the number of ounces by 30.)

1 oz	=	⅟₁₆ lb	=	30 g
4 oz	=	¼ lb	=	120 g
8 oz	=	½ lb	=	240 g
12 oz	=	¾ lb	=	360 g
16 oz	=	1 lb	=	480 g

Useful Equivalents for Length

(To convert inches to centimeters, multiply the number of inches by 2.5.)

1 in					=	2.5 cm		
6 in	=	½ ft			=	15 cm		
12 in	=	1 ft			=	30 cm		
36 in	=	3 ft	=	1 yd	=	90 cm		
40 in					=	100 cm	=	1 m

Useful Equivalents for Liquid Ingredients by Volume

¼ tsp					=	1 ml	
½ tsp					=	2 ml	
1 tsp					=	5 ml	
3 tsp	=	1 Tbsp			=	½ fl oz	=	15 ml
		2 Tbsp	=	⅛ cup	=	1 fl oz	=	30 ml
		4 Tbsp	=	¼ cup	=	2 fl oz	=	60 ml
		5⅓ Tbsp	=	⅓ cup	=	3 fl oz	=	80 ml
		8 Tbsp	=	½ cup	=	4 fl oz	=	120 ml
		10⅔ Tbsp	=	⅔ cup	=	5 fl oz	=	160 ml
		12 Tbsp	=	¾ cup	=	6 fl oz	=	180 ml
		16 Tbsp	=	1 cup	=	8 fl oz	=	240 ml
		1 pt	=	2 cups	=	16 fl oz	=	480 ml
		1 qt	=	4 cups	=	32 fl oz	=	960 ml
						33 fl oz	=	1000 ml = 1 l

Useful Equivalents for Cooking/Oven Temperatures

	Fahrenheit	Celsius	Gas Mark
Freeze water	32° F	0° C	
Room temperature	68° F	20° C	
Boil water	212° F	100° C	
Bake	325° F	160° C	3
	350° F	180° C	4
	375° F	190° C	5
	400° F	200° C	6
	425° F	220° C	7
	450° F	230° C	8
Broil			Grill

Index

Hotel and Restaurant Index

★ = Morgan's Favorite   ◼ = Hotel

Acknowledgments

I'm grateful to my colleagues at Time Inc. and Oxmoor House—Jim Childs, Daniel Fagan, Leigh Sloss Cora, and especially to my editor, Nichole Aksamit. Thanks to the Oxmoor House Test Kitchen staff for not burning me on high heat in effigy every time I sent in a recipe that was designed to feed 2,000 people or originally prepared in a 25-gallon vat. A special thank-you goes to four very brilliant interns and fellow Oxonians, who traveled mile upon mile with me in search of culinary greatness over a stretch of two hot Southern summers: the indefatigable Frances Girling, insatiable Cicely Hadman, ever-buoyant Alicia Luba, and wry Emma McNulty. Lastly, and most important, I'm deeply indebted and humbled by those restaurateurs who dedicate themselves to feeding their communities and enriching our lives with their creativity in the kitchen. I wish you full plates, glasses, tables, and hearts.

About the Author

Don't believe in gentlemen? Spend an hour with Morgan Murphy. The best-selling author and vintage car enthusiast wears impeccably tailored suits and polished shoes to dinner, habits picked up during his years at Oxford University and service to the U.S. Navy. He stands when a woman approaches. And when his blue eyes twinkle and his cheeks dimple, a hilarious tale is sure to follow. Murphy is the author of the original *Off the Eaten Path* cookbook and co-author of *I Love You—Now Hush*. His trademark wit has appeared in *Vanity Fair*, *Forbes*, *Esquire*, *The New York Post*, and *Southern Living*, where he served as travel editor, food critic, and national spokesman. Often called "America's funniest food critic," he has appeared on the *TODAY* show, *Fox & Friends*, *CNN*, Sirius/XM, and National Public Radio. There's some iron behind his cigar smoke. Murphy serves as a lieutenant commander in the U.S. Navy and is a veteran of the war in Afghanistan. He lives in Birmingham, Alabama, with his old dog, Gilbert.

Southern Living

Off the Eaten Path

Favorite Southern Dives and 150 Recipes
That Made Them Famous

by Morgan Murphy

foreword by
Fannie Flagg

Praise for the Original

"Now that Off the Eaten Path is in place in the backseat of my Buick, I'm ready for my next road trip through God's country."

—Pat Conroy, author of
The Prince of Tides and South of Broad

"Morgan Murphy shows how, with a little effort and guidance, you can experience the South like a true Southerner."

—Fox News

"We are thrilled that Morgan Murphy has tracked down these recipes so we can have them in the comfort of home."

—Jane and Michael Stern,
authors of Roadfood and
The Lexicon of Real American Food

"Morgan Murphy knows firsthand about some of the best-kept Southern secrets in the culinary world."

—NBC's TODAY show

"The treasured recipes, the roundabout routes, the out-of-the-way places, and porch-rocking stories—I love everything about this delightful book!"

—Cassandra King, author of
The Same Sweet Girls and Queen of Broken Hearts

"[Morgan Murphy] keeps a schedule that makes us feel like the biggest slackers ever to inhabit a BarcaLounger."

—NPR's Car Talk

"Morgan Murphy, former Southern Living travel editor, food critic, Navy reservist, and admirer of vintage Cadillacs, is a certified road-tripper — if such things were certified."

—Chicago Tribune